BETRAYED

The shocking story
of two undercover cops

BETRAYED

Clive Small and Tom Gilling

ALLEN&UNWIN

Allen & Unwin
83 Alexander Street
Crows Nest NSW 2065
Australia
Phone: (61 2) 8425 0100
Fax: (61 2) 9906 2218
Email: info@allenandunwin.com
Web: www.allenandunwin.com

Cataloguing-in-Publication details are available
from the National Library of Australia
www.librariesaustralia.nla.gov.au

ISBN 978 1 74175 963 1

Internal design by Darian Causby
Set in Sabon 11/18 pt Sabon by Midland Typesetters, Australia

10 9 8 7 6 5 4 3 2 1

To Joe and Jessie's parents, family and friends,
who never let them down

Contents

Preface

This is the story of two people who joined the New South Wales Police thinking they could make a difference. For reasons of personal and family safety their real names cannot be used: we'll call them Joe and Jessie, although they have used a number of aliases.

Joe and Jessie live with their young twins in Sydney's western suburbs. They met as undercover cops, trusting each other with their lives as they infiltrated a world of drugs, guns and violence. In order to blend into that world, they had to be part of it. They were cops pretending to be crooks. Their targets were not only criminals but corrupt police.

The work was exciting, and Joe and Jessie were good at it. Ambitious but inexperienced, they threw themselves into their fictional roles believing that the people in charge, the senior commanders who ran operations from the safety of police headquarters, knew the difference between crooked cops and honest cops pretending to be crooked.

They were wrong.

Acknowledgements

Our sincere thanks to those former undercover cops who have been willing to speak to us about their experiences, and to the journalists and former police who helped expose a flawed system.

About the authors

In 2009 Clive Small and Tom Gilling published the bestselling book *Smack Express: How organised crime got hooked on drugs,* which exposed the growth and transformation of organised crime in Australia since the late 1960s. They followed this in 2010 with *Blood Money: Bikies, terrorists and Middle Eastern gangs.*

Clive Small is a 38-year New South Wales police veteran. Much of his time was spent in criminal investigation. He was awarded several commendations. From 1977 to 1980 he worked as an investigator with the Woodward Royal Commission into Drug Trafficking. During 1987–88 he was an investigator on Strike Force Omega, which reinvestigated the 1984 shooting of Detective Michael Drury. In the early 1990s Small led the backpacker murder investigation which resulted in the conviction of Ivan Robert Milat for the murder of seven backpackers in Belanglo State Forest, south of Sydney, between 1989 and 1992. In 2001, as head of the Greater Hume Police Region, he helped dismantle the Vietnamese street gangs that had made Cabramatta Australia's heroin capital. After retiring from the police he joined the NSW Independent Commission Against Corruption as the Executive Director of Operations. Since March 2007 he has been writing full time.

Tom Gilling's first two novels, *The Sooterkin* (1999) and *Miles McGinty* (2001), were both shortlisted for major awards and chosen as notable books of the year by the *New York Times*. They have been translated into several languages. His third novel, *Dreamland* (2008), has been published in Australia, Britain and the United States. As a journalist he has worked for numerous publications including the *Sydney Morning Herald*, *The Australian*, *The Bulletin*, *The Guardian* (UK), *The Observer* (UK) and the *New York Times*. Before *Smack Express*, he wrote two non-fiction books, *Trial and Error* (1991, revised 1995), about the Israeli nuclear whistleblower Mordechai Vanunu, and *Bagman: The final confessions of Jack Herbert* (2005), about the events that led to the Fitzgerald Commission into police corruption in Queensland.

Chapter 1
Beginnings

There is nothing inside or outside the two-storey house in Sydney's west that identifies its owners as former members of the New South Wales Police. The plaques and academy photos that once hung proudly at Joe's parents' home have long since been taken down. Even within the family, their time in the police force is never spoken about. The careers of two undercover cops who put several dangerous criminals and a handful of drug-dealing detectives behind bars are now, in Joe's words, nothing more than a 'bad memory'.

If he happened to bump into one of his old underworld contacts, it's unlikely they would recognise him. Joe has become used to denying the person he was, even to himself.

He would look them in the eye and tell them they were mistaken, and in the end they would believe him. In any case, Joe looks nothing like the person he was: the flashy drug dealer, the gym junkie with three gold hoops in each ear and a diamond stud. Gone is the long braided hair, the colourful suits, the jewellery, the expensive car. Joe has lost 30 kilos and shuffles about most days in a tracksuit and thongs.

A photograph on the fridge shows him posing beside champion bodybuilder Ronnie Coleman, an eight-time Mr Olympia. Joe works out every morning in his home gym, but without the steroids that messed with his mind and wrecked his kidneys. His upper body is covered in tattoos. He still radiates a kind of menace, even wearing thongs and pushing a pram.

The change in Jessie's appearance is less obvious. To the neighbours and the people she meets when she is out shopping, Jessie is just a mum with young twins to look after. She doesn't want them to think anything else.

Life for Joe and Jessie looks comfortable enough but they have struggled to cope with what happened to them. As undercover cops they survived on instinct and ability, with little of the experience that would have equipped them to handle the psychological pressures of the job. It wasn't just criminals they had to deceive but friends, and even family. Nobody told them how hard it would be to live with the lies they had told while working undercover. Lies they told, lies they had to tell, both to protect themselves and each other, have never been forgiven.

People they know—like the plumber who has convinced himself that Joe is a bikie—will read their story without realising it is about them. Most of the criminals they helped put in jail have now been released. Some of them might recognise Joe and Jessie, but not as the people they are now—a young married couple in Sydney's western suburbs with kids, a car and a mortgage.

This was not the future Joe's conservative Muslim parents imagined for their son when they migrated to Australia in 1973, although their own lives had been far from easy. As children and later as young adults, Joe's father and mother were caught up in the chaos that shaped Lebanon and Palestine in the decades after the Second World War. Joe's father (we will call him Mohammad) was born in Tripoli, Lebanon, in 1940, the second of nine children. The family were practising Muslims. Mohammad's father worked as a butcher while his mother looked after the children. It was a hard life but Mohammad did well at school. After completing the equivalent of Year 12 he worked at various jobs, eventually becoming a teacher's aide at a primary school.

Like many other Lebanese Muslims of his generation, Mohammad had grown up with a strong sympathy for the Palestinians, many of whom had been driven out of Israel to an uncertain future as refugees in neighbouring countries. As a young man Mohammad took a passionate interest in the Israeli–Palestinian conflict and became a political activist against what he saw as Israeli aggression.

Joe's mother (we will call her Salma) was born into a Muslim family in Palestine in 1946, the eldest of five children. Her father worked as a policeman for the British government that would administer the country for another two years. When the first Arab–Israeli war broke out on the termination of the Mandate on 15 May 1948 the family was forced out of their home. For several years they lived in a refugee camp near Ramallah on the central West Bank of Palestine before being allowed to migrate to Lebanon.

Jobs and money were scarce for Palestinian immigrants and, along with thousands of other families, they struggled to survive. As Salma recalls, 'My father was a good man, but he never recovered from losing his job, his home, and his country. I think he died of a broken heart.'

Mohammad and Salma met in the streets of Tripoli in 1960 and married a few months later. In 1961, at the age of twenty-one, Mohammad became an intelligence operative for the Egyptian government which, as the major regional power, recruited agents from all over the Middle East. Since 1958 Syria and Egypt had been merged as the United Arab Republic, but the union collapsed in 1961 after a military coup in Syria. The following year Mohammad secretly entered Syria to meet with members of the deposed Syrian government in an attempt to identify plotters based in Egypt. In Syria he was arrested and beaten before being released. Mohammad was lucky—the Syrian agents had nothing on him and saw no reason to hold him. He never returned to Syria but continued to work on covert operations in Egypt and Lebanon.

In 1964 Mohammad went to work for the Lebanese government, becoming a field operative for the *mokhabarat*— the secret police. The job guaranteed a modest income and a degree of protection from the government, but it came with its own risks: if his job became known or if the regime changed, his entire family would be in danger. In order to protect his parents and family, Mohammad never told them what he did. As far as they knew he simply worked for the government. They did not ask questions.

Mohammad's work took him to Jordan, Iraq and Egypt. He always worked with male partners and carried a gun. In 1965, as Mohammad and two fellow agents left a cabaret club in Beirut, a man stepped from the crowd and pulled a handgun. As bystanders panicked and ran, the man fired at Mohammad and his colleagues from a distance of only five metres. The hit was so quick that none of them had time to draw their weapons. Mohammad escaped unhurt but both his companions were shot in the chest—one fatally. The killer was of Arabic appearance, about thirty-five years old, and wearing western clothes. After firing five shots, he calmly turned around and disappeared into the crowd. It was a political assassination: the agents discovered later that their covers had been blown.

This was the only time a direct attempt was made on Mohammad's life, but as an undercover agent in one of the most corrupt and unstable regions in the world he knew that the threat of assassination was ever-present.

Mohammad and others spent five months on the surveillance of a spy working in Beirut for the Israeli government. The spy, who was masquerading as an Arab businessman, was gathering street-level intelligence about attitudes towards the government as well as fomenting unrest where possible. On several occasions he caught a boat to Cyprus and was followed all the way to Israel. Surveillance stopped at the Israeli border—the risks of operating inside Israel were too great. Just before the spy was arrested, his apartment was searched. The searchers found false passports and forged papers supporting his cover story, as well as notes of intelligence he had gathered and reported back to his handlers. He was detained and interrogated before being returned to Israel as part of a political deal.

By the early 1970s Lebanon was sliding towards the civil war that would eventually erupt in 1975, bringing with it the collapse of law and order. Mohammad knew that in the faction-ridden world of Lebanese politics his work with the secret police put him in extreme danger, and that if he was arrested, his family would pay the price. He wanted to get out but his employment prospects looked bleak. His years with the *mokhabarat* had given him skills that were of little use except, perhaps, in the murky Lebanese underworld of crime and corruption.

Mere survival was a constant struggle in a once-prosperous country that was now critically short of doctors and decent hospitals. By now Mohammad's wife had given birth to ten children—including two sets of twins—eight of whom had died before the age of two. The children were born in the family apartment with the help of a self-taught midwife who lived in the same block. Mohammad realised that the only future for his family lay outside Lebanon.

A few years earlier one of Mohammad's sisters had migrated with her family to Australia and settled in Melbourne. One of Salma's brothers had also migrated to Australia, settling in Sydney. Both seemed to love their adopted country, a place where hard work was rewarded and families were free to live without the constant fear of war. Mohammad applied for his family to join them but the process was arduous and there were seemingly interminable bureaucratic delays both in Lebanon and Australia.

In late 1973 permission was suddenly granted for Mohammad and his family to emigrate. But there was a problem. Joe, who was born on 25 June 1973, was not included on the migration papers. His mother had only fallen pregnant with Joe after the application had been submitted. His parents were terrified that if they tried to change their application to include Joe, their permission to enter Australia might be revoked and the whole process would have to start again. Worse, they feared that with civil war looming any delay might cost them the only chance they had to leave Lebanon. In the end they felt they had no choice but to leave baby Joe behind with relatives. As soon as the rest of the family was safely in Australia, they would make arrangements for Joe to join them.

The family—Mohammad, Salma and their two daughters—settled in Sydney's south-west in what was then a small and close-knit Muslim-Arabic community. They were happy to be in Australia but Salma was tormented by guilt at having left her only son behind. Her one comfort was the knowledge that their relatives back in Lebanon would look after him.

It took nearly a year to obtain the necessary documents for Joe. Mohammad and Salma now faced the biggest obstacle of all: collecting Joe from Lebanon and bringing him to Australia. Because Mohammad had been a member of the secret police it was far too risky for either Mohammad or Salma to fetch him in person, but who else could they trust? By chance a member of their extended family in

Sydney was preparing to visit relatives in Lebanon. He asked if there was anything he could bring back for them. 'The only thing I need, God willing, is my baby,' Salma remembers saying.

In Lebanon, the relative tracked down the one-year-old baby Joe. Mohammad and Salma had given him all the official papers but leaving the country with someone else's baby was no easy task, and nor was getting the child into Australia. Meanwhile, Salma waited and prayed. She had already suffered the loss of eight children; being separated from Joe was almost more than she could bear. She and Mohammad knew the flight he was booked on but they hardly dared hope that Joe was on his way to Australia. At the sight of their baby being carried through the arrivals gate, both parents were overcome with emotion. Reunited at last, Salma vowed never to abandon her son again.

With the family together at last, Joe's parents could turn their thoughts to establishing themselves in their new country. Both found jobs in local factories and after five years they had saved enough money to buy the house they still live in today. As well as two older sisters, Joe now had a younger sister and brother born in Australia. His mother gave up work to look after the family. After fifteen years working in factories, Mohammad left to set up his own business, trading goods within the Arabic community—a job from which he has only recently retired.

Raised in the Bankstown area, Joe went to a local public school and mixed with a group of Lebanese youths, mostly Muslims, that included future gang leaders Adnan Darwiche and Abdul Razzak, their brothers and cousins. Among a wider network of friends was another future criminal, Michael Kanaan. Between them, these three would be responsible for much of the violence that swept across south-west Sydney during the late 1990s and early 2000s—an orgy of murder and intimidation that, for a while, the police seemed powerless to stop.

Like others his age, Joe felt the pressure to join the emerging gangs. At the same time he admired his father, whom he knew as a 'policeman in Lebanon', and wanted to be like him. In his late teens, as he completed his schooling, Joe worked part time as a shop assistant, store security guard and model. He watched some of his friends heading down the road to crime and saw their contempt for the police. He also witnessed the other side: police treating young Muslim men as if they were criminals simply for being Muslim. Joe saw the hostility this engendered. He witnessed Muslim women and young girls being treated with disrespect. It was a destructive cycle and perhaps, Joe thought, he could do something about it.

In 1992, at the age of eighteen, he joined the New South Wales Police. Later that year he was sworn in as a probationary constable. At the time there were precious few practising Muslims in the New South Wales Police. Joe's family and many in the broader Lebanese Muslim community were proud of him, not only for his own achievement but also for the respect he had brought to the community. Joe recalls the day of the swearing-in as 'the happiest of my life', but in the years to come the confidence he had in his chosen career was to prove horribly misplaced.

For the next three years Joe worked the streets of Wetherill Park and Fairfield in Sydney's south-west. For a period he was assigned to the locally created Special Operations Group, which was set up primarily to target the Vietnamese street gangs and heroin markets of Cabramatta. Joe walked the streets in casual clothes, talking to drug dealers, gathering intelligence and evidence, and identifying possible targets for police swoops. It was during this period that his potential as an undercover operative first came to the notice of his superiors. In mid-1995 Joe was approached by then Detective Inspector Steve Matthews, chief of detectives at Fairfield local area command and a highly experienced drug investigator. Matthews recalls: 'I had seen him work the streets and he was pretty good. He had that ability to mix easily and talk to the crooks. I thought he would make a good undercover operative so I made a few phone calls.'

Joe was interested and appeared before a selection panel of undercover experts who assessed him as suitable for the Drug Enforcement Agency's undercover unit, which had overall responsibility for undercover operations throughout the New South Wales Police Force. The decision to centralise undercover operations with the DEA acknowledged the fact that undercover operations in New South Wales had begun as a response to the explosion in drug use in the late 1960s. For years the DEA's effective ownership of undercover policing had put it largely beyond the reach of detectives investigating other areas of crime. This exclusivity led to the ad hoc growth of undercover units during the 1980s and 1990s. Neither training nor supervision was standardised and it was only in 1988 that specialist training for undercover police was introduced. Although drugs remained the priority of the DEA's undercover unit, it would also undertake investigations into homicide, armed robbery and major property theft.

Joe's interview panel included Detective Michael Drury, who, as an undercover cop a decade earlier, had been shot through a window and seriously wounded while standing in the kitchen of his Chatswood home. The shooter was the Melbourne hitman Christopher Dale Flannery, who later was murdered on the orders of organised crime 'godfathers' Lennie McPherson and George Freeman.

Another member of the panel was Detective Paul Jones, who, four years later, as a detective superintendent at Crime Agencies, led strike forces Portville and Scottsville in a clean-up of the street gangs, violence and heroin markets of Cabramatta. Between 1999 and mid-2001 these two strike forces made around one hundred arrests and laid more than one hundred and sixty charges, including six of murder, eight of conspiracy to murder and thirty-one of firearms possession, together with numerous others relating to drug supply and possession.

The interview panel was not easy on its subjects. They began by questioning Joe about his life before he joined the police, looking for ways his background could be built into a cover story. They also questioned him in detail about his experiences as a police officer in order to determine whether his career so far might already have compromised a future role in undercover work. Among the questions Joe was asked were: how well known was he in criminal circles as a police officer? What exposure had he had to major criminals? What capacity had he demonstrated to be able to act under pressure? Was he able to think quickly on his feet? His answers to all these questions enabled the interview panel to assess his suitability to work undercover.

Joe was then presented with different scenarios he might encounter as a policeman and asked how he would react. This led to an impromptu role-playing exercise in which Joe was told to assume he was undercover and had to enter a hotel known to be frequented by criminals and make a drug buy from one of them. One of the panel was identified as the drug dealer. Joe was given instructions which he was told to follow for his own safety.

What he was not told was that the 'drug dealer' would be attempting to lure him into unacceptable high-risk situations. Central to the test was Joe's ability to identify these risks and avoid them. Joe realised that it was a test of his ability to ad lib in situations and that the more successful he was the tougher the scenario would become: the twists and turns would increase and there would be pressure for him to take greater risks. For example, he might be told, 'I've only got a couple of grams of heroin, but the bloke I deal for has got a couple of ounces. He's in the car out the back. Come for a walk and we'll see him.' He was being offered a bigger heroin seizure and a bigger potential arrest, but he was also being taken out of the safety zone—the hotel—to a place where he would be vulnerable to a rip-off or worse.

Joe knew that the first time he made a mistake, the panel could declare, 'You're dead.' The scenario went for about half an hour—it seemed much longer—but by the end Joe thought he had done all right. Although hesitant at the start, he felt he had grown in confidence as the exercise continued.

Whatever Joe thought about his own performance, the panel was impressed. Out of a hundred applicants, Joe was one of ten selected for the live-in training course during which he and the others would be tested day and night over ten days. In many ways the course was an extension of the panel interview. It included risk identification and management, scenarios and role-playing, and studying the law to learn what

undercover police could and could not do. The course was run
by Detective Drury, who would later say of Joe's performance,
'He displayed the skills and ability to work within the field
at a high level.' In late 1995 Joe was transferred to the Drug
Enforcement Agency's undercover unit.

*

Jessie's childhood was very different to Joe's. She was born in
Perth, Western Australia, in 1972. She has four sisters—one
is her twin—and a brother. Her father worked in real estate
while her mother was a nurse before designing and making
clothing for her own children's boutiques. The family was
quite well off when Jessie was young but as a result of
some bad business decisions her parents got into financial
difficulties and their businesses were forced to close. In 1984
her parents moved to Queensland and settled on the Gold
Coast. The following year her parents separated.

Their separation had a traumatic effect on Jessie. Her
behaviour at home and at school deteriorated and she was
finally expelled. After moving to another school Jessie
began looking for part-time jobs, starting as a dishwasher
and kitchen hand and eventually working as a waitress in
a Chinese restaurant. Both parents had instilled a strong
work ethic in their children: Jessie remembers it as almost
a substitute for religion. At the end of Year 12 Jessie left
school.

Comparing her family with Joe's, Jessie sees the profound cultural differences: 'Me and my brother and sisters, and most of our friends, left home quite young, mainly to attend college and uni. We lived with friends and travelled. But in Joe's family and other Muslim families you only leave home to get married. Family is the top priority.'

In 1992 Jessie and her twin sister moved to Sydney. Jessie worked in western Sydney as a bar manager while completing an Associate Diploma in Fine Arts. One day she was pulled over by a police officer. The officer was in an unmarked police car, casually dressed and (as Jessie later found out) under suspension over a domestic violence incident. Ordering her to get out of the car, he told Jessie that the music in her car was too loud. His manner was aggressive and threatening. When Jessie protested, he grabbed her arm and pushed her.

It was not the first time Jessie had been bullied by the police. Five years earlier she and two friends had been assaulted by drunken police on the Gold Coast. Jessie and her mother reported the incident to the Broadbeach police, but they showed little interest in following up her complaint. Later Jessie's mother received a letter from the Broadbeach police saying that the matter had been fully investigated but they had been unable to identify the officers involved. For some, that report would have been the last straw. But Jessie had been brought up to obey the law and to respect the police. She saw both incidents as exceptions to the sort of conduct she expected from the police: evidence not of something wrong in the institution but rather of isolated behavioural problems that could and should be fixed.

The thought of joining the police began to form in her mind almost without Jessie knowing it. She was nearing the end of her studies and had no job to go to. She had seen individual officers abusing their power but this had not diminished her faith in the police as a whole. Her own brushes with the law made her think that she had something to offer.

In 1994 Jessie applied for and was accepted into the New South Wales Police Force. Sworn in as a probationary constable, she began uniformed duties at Wetherill Park. By coincidence it was the same station Joe had been assigned to, although by the time Jessie arrived, Joe had already left.

After Wetherill Park, Jessie was transferred to Penrith to complete her training. It was during her time at Penrith that Jessie had her first taste of working undercover. She was asked to pose as a prostitute on the Great Western Highway in Kingswood. Jessie's task was to lure men over to ask about prices and then to arrest them for soliciting. She wasn't wired but surveillance was always close by. As undercover jobs went this one was pretty routine, but Jessie found the experience exciting: 'It might sound corny, but it gave me a different view of policing. I realised for the first time that in order to catch people who are breaking the law, you sometimes have to put yourself in their position, to think like them. You can't stop crime just by walking around in a blue uniform and carrying a gun.'

After a few months Jessie was transferred to Kogarah local area command where she spent the next two years working general duties. She also began studying for her Bachelor of Social Science (Criminal Justice) degree which she would complete several years later.

The role-playing at Penrith had whetted her interest in undercover work and Jessie was eager for another chance, but as a junior constable her opportunities were limited. In one operation Jessie dressed as a schoolgirl at a local high school in Kogarah to help catch a flasher who was indecently exposing himself to students as they walked to and from the school. A suspect was caught after one of the students managed to write down a number plate. The man worked in a bank not far from Kogarah police station. Although he was a serial flasher, the police only charged him with three indecent exposure offences.

When the case went to court the magistrate noted that it was an 'identification case' and that the identification was strong. Several witnesses picked the suspect in a photo line-up, but after the wife of the accused swore on oath that her husband was with her at the time one offence was committed, the magistrate had to dismiss all the charges.

'It was another useful lesson,' according to Jessie. 'Getting a case to court is only half the battle. The other half is securing a conviction. You can't stop people lying to get themselves out of trouble but if you can find enough evidence to show that a person has committed a crime then lying won't save them. You can't win every time but if you've got enough evidence then chances are you'll get a result.'

In 1997 Jessie switched to full-time criminal investigation work at Kogarah and began training to become a detective. It wouldn't be long before she was formally recruited to work undercover.

Chapter 2

Joe goes undercover

In 1995, while Jessie was finding her feet as a police officer in Sydney's western suburbs, Joe began his new life as an undercover cop in the Drug Enforcement Agency (DEA). The following year the DEA's undercover team was transferred to the Special Services Group, which was to assume responsibility for providing undercover support for all police covert operations and standardising recruitment and training for covert operatives. Joe's duties didn't change; as far as he was concerned he still worked for the drug squad.

Joe's one handicap in working undercover was that he was a Muslim. Christian Lebanese criminals have long had a role in Sydney's underworld. It began more than forty years ago with the emergence of the first Lebanese godfather, Faycz 'Frank' Hakim. Hakim was about twenty when he arrived in Australia. During the late 1950s and early 1960s he built an extensive social network among the Lebanese community, helping many, and became a prominent member of the community.

Hakim's interest in gambling led him to form an alliance with police at the infamous No. 21 Special Squad, which at that time had responsibility for enforcing the gambling laws. By the early 1960s they had established a lucrative partnership. Within a decade Hakim was a central figure in a corrupt network headed by Leonard Arthur McPherson and George David Freeman, the two 'Mr Bigs' of organised crime. Under the noses of the police, Freeman and McPherson provided protection to ethnic-based illegal gambling clubs, casinos, illegal starting price bookmakers and vice operations. For a quarter of a century Hakim was the figurehead of Lebanese organised crime in Sydney. By the time he died in 2005 at the age of seventy-five he had relinquished his role as a godfather. Other Lebanese criminals had emerged to take his place, including Louis and Billy Bayeh.

The power of the Bayeh crime family declined as a direct result of the investigations and exposures of the 1994–97 Wood Royal Commission into the New South Wales Police Service. Out of the vacuum two Lebanese crime gangs emerged to spread intimidation and violence in an arc from Kings Cross to Sydney's south-west and western suburbs. The first gang was led by Danny Karam and known as DK's Boys. The second was led by Michael Kanaan, a former member of Karam's gang who took over after he and others murdered Karam. One of the reasons for Karam's murder was his poor treatment of the Muslim members of his own gang. A brief lull followed the jailing of Kanaan before violence erupted again between rival gangs led by Adnan Darwiche and Abdul Razzak.

As the dominant force in Sydney's Middle Eastern underworld, Lebanese Christian gangs—unlike their Muslim rivals—had established strong and profitable criminal connections with non-Middle Eastern gangs. As a Muslim, Joe would have had problems ingratiating himself with the broader criminal milieu.

Working as an undercover among mainly Lebanese Christian criminals meant Joe had to 'convert'. His Muslim upbringing would be erased: from now on he would be a Christian. The names he took were western. The cover name 'Joe', chosen by the authors, was used during several operations. Joe's conversion also meant he began to drink alcohol and smoke. He stopped attending his mosque. He wore flashy clothes and associated with equally flashy women, visiting nightclubs and other places that he had previously shunned.

The changes were not immediate but cumulative as Joe began to take on the life and trappings of a 'bad boy':

Staying away from the mosque helped me to avoid questions about what I was doing and the changes in my appearance. Nobody ordered me not to go to the mosque but I suppose I was just falling in line with the story I had been telling other people. That's how I justified the drinking and smoking. I was telling myself that it wasn't me, it was the person I was pretending to be. It was Joe and Joe had to do it. It was part of the act and I still believe I wouldn't have got the arrests I did without smoking and drinking. Soon it just became a part of my life and I stopped thinking about it. By then it wasn't just Joe turning his back on Muslim values, it was me.

Pitting religion against career was a challenge few, if any, of Joe's undercover colleagues had ever had to make. Like all undercover police, Joe was worried about being recognised, particularly when working in south-west Sydney, but he was careful to check out the targets he was assigned and as a fallback he always had his cover story: that he had changed his name after being sacked as a corrupt cop as a result of the Wood Royal Commission.

Over the next two years Joe undertook more than a dozen undercover jobs. At times he was working on as many as three different operations simultaneously. As well as drugs he investigated the sale of stolen property and weapons. The jobs took him to many parts of the state including Coffs Harbour, Port Macquarie, Gunnedah, Albury, Bourke, Wollongong and Newcastle. The drugs involved ranged from cannabis to amphetamines, speed, ecstasy, heroin and steroids. Joe made use of intelligence gathered from informants and from other investigations; he talked unsuspecting lower-level dealers into introducing him to higher-level dealers who were the targets of the operation; he depended on planning, initiative and, on occasion, luck. Most assignments went off without a hitch. But not all.

Joe had always looked after his body; he had, after all, sometimes worked as a model. When he began undercover work he was broad shouldered and slim, weighing 82 kilograms. Although he was fit and healthy and stood 184 centimetres tall, this wasn't the build of a tough guy and underworld enforcer. In order to look the part he started working out in the kind of gyms known to be frequented by the heavies of Sydney's underworld—the people whose networks Joe was required to infiltrate. Over time he befriended the gym regulars and was introduced to steroids. Joe couldn't help being impressed by these 'gym junkies'. He saw how big they were and how much respect they commanded in the gym. 'I remember thinking,' he says, 'that bulking up with steroids would gain me the same respect and that the extra size would be a kind of protection.'

Soon Joe was using steroids heavily. His use of the drug and the time he spent in the gym gave plenty of credibility to the cover story that he was a bodyguard and sometime standover man who was active in the drug trade. Joe's professional confidence increased along with his size. He knew that others would think twice before hassling him. 'Sometimes,' he recalls, 'I would be doing two jobs at the same time—one in the morning on one target and another in the afternoon or evening on another.' He believes he could not have kept up the routine, or put on the necessary weight, without using steroids.

Joe had expected undercover work to focus on the drug trade but one of his first jobs was a major investigation into stolen property. This would turn out to be an important learning experience. In late 1995 Joe was introduced to Patrick, a well-known criminal and conman from Sydney's eastern suburbs. In his late twenties, clean shaven and with a liking for expensive suits, Patrick used to describe himself as an 'entrepreneur'. In Joe's words he was a 'flash rat'. Patrick claimed to have one hundred and eighty Nokia mobile phones for sale. Joe expressed an interest in buying them but it seemed he was too late: Patrick already had a buyer. Like most things in the underworld, however, it became clear that there was room for negotiation. The phones could be Joe's, Patrick said, provided he came up with a better offer.

Over the next two months offers and counter offers were made but it was obvious that Patrick was trying to play the two buyers off against each other, and that nothing he said could be trusted. In his efforts to keep Joe interested, Patrick kept adding to his original story. Eventually he said something that could be checked and shown to be false. Near the end of February the operation was abruptly cancelled when it turned out that Patrick did not have any phones to sell. He was simply trying to pull a rip-off. It was a valuable lesson for Joe. For Patrick, the decision to cancel the operation meant he survived to put another deal to a new sucker. Patrick was later arrested by other police in an unrelated scam.

It was only a matter of days before Joe was assigned to another job. This one did involve drugs. For the first time it gave Joe an opportunity to start near the street level of an illegal drug network and work his way up to the big dealers.

In March 1996 he infiltrated a group supplying steroids in Sydney. The amounts were relatively small but the business made good money. Joe explained that he had just moved back to Sydney after some time in Brisbane where he had worked as a bodyguard for some strippers and sold drugs on the side. He had a fair bit of cash, he told them, and was interested in getting into the big time in Sydney.

Keen to get their hands on some of Joe's money, the dealers were quick to arrange an introduction to their supplier, John (not his real name). In mid-April Joe met John, who was based at Coffs Harbour, at the Mooney Tavern. Over a few drinks, Joe told John his cover story and outlined his plans. What he was proposing was a bit big for John. The man to see, he told Joe, was Roy (short for steroids and not his real name), who was the major supplier of steroids in the area. Roy had a record for receiving stolen property and drugs supply. As well as steroids, he also supplied ecstasy.

A couple of days later, on 18 April, Joe met John at Argyle Place, Coffs Harbour. John made a telephone call and a few moments later Roy pulled up in a white Ford sedan. Roy was in his late twenties, Caucasian, with a bulky steroid-enhanced physique, very short hair and a diamond stud in each ear. 'He dressed like a surfer,' Joe recalls, 'with multicoloured beach pants, a white singlet, baseball cap and sandals.'

After introductions Roy got straight down to business: 'What [type of steroids] do you want? ... Anything you want I can get.' The price would depend how much Joe wanted to buy. When Joe asked about ecstasy Roy replied, 'No, I don't do that shit. Two guys got busted last week for two kilos of speed and things are really hot. There's too much risk involved in that. With steroids you can have a truck load and get caught and all they'll give you is a fine.' ·

They started talking prices. Roy said, 'I have a guy who takes two hundred to two fifty [ten millilitre] bottles [at a time] and gives me $30 to $35 each.'

As always, Joe had known the going rate before they started talking. The Drug Enforcement Agency regularly collected drug prices and kept its undercover police informed (see Appendix 1). The price Roy had quoted was about right. 'What have you got now?' Joe asked.

Roy offered to sell him a 50 ml bottle for $150 but said it would take about five minutes to get it. 'Okay,' said Joe. 'I'll take it back to Sydney. When I'm down there I'll take orders then contact you and give you time to organise it … One large amount will be worth the drive up.'

Joe was pleased with the way things had gone. He had made a buy already and there was a bigger deal in the offing. Roy would have been happy about making a quick sale and finding a new customer who appeared to have ready access to cash.

After returning to Sydney Joe spent a couple of weeks negotiating further deals with Roy. The bottle he bought sold quickly, he assured Roy. It was good quality and stronger than the steroids available in Sydney, the buyer had told him. If the stuff they had been talking about was of the same quality, Joe would be interested in buying fifteen hundred bottles; he had a mate, he said, who would take a lot of it off his hands. They agreed on a price of $27 a bottle for the first consignment. Future sales for a similar amount once a month would be a bit cheaper: $25 a bottle.

Roy promised to have the steroids in about a week. A couple of days later Joe confirmed the order. 'Everything looks good so far,' Roy told him. 'I'm just getting them together.' But Roy had spoken too soon. Getting his hands on such a large quantity was harder than he'd expected. It took him nearly a month to get hold of three hundred bottles. Another three hundred had been promised, but they were a few days away.

Joe made his way to Coffs Harbour. On the morning of 16 May he called Roy to arrange a meeting. Roy now had three hundred and thirty bottles which he would sell for $27 a bottle. Joe had $10,000 cash to make the buy.

At about 10 am Joe drove into the McDonald's parking lot on the Pacific Highway and waited. Three-quarters of an hour later a Holden with Victorian plates pulled alongside. Roy was sitting in the passenger seat. Joe did not recognise the driver.

Joe got out of his car, leaned into the Holden through the passenger-side window and shook hands.

'How are you, Roy?'

'Good, mate,' he replied.

'How's everything?'

'Good.'

'How many have you got?'

'Three hundred and thirty bottles.'

Joe looked at the driver but Roy did not introduce him, although he referred to him as Alex (not his real name).

'What's in them?' asked Joe.

'All sorts, mate. We've got Deca, Filybol and Probolin ... It's a mixture of everything ... About forty to fifty bottles of each.' (Deca-Durabolin is used to build muscle while Filybol and Probolin are veterinary steroids that have to be mixed with other steroids for muscle gain. Bodybuilders use all three.)

'Have you got them with you?' Joe asked.

'No,' Roy replied. 'But they're nearby. Look, mate, I know there has been some stuffing around in getting it. But I'll have one thousand [bottles] next week. Follow us.'

Joe was nervous. The agreement had been that the deal would be done in the McDonald's car park and that it would be between him and Roy. But now there were two of them— one of whom Joe had never seen before—and he was being told the location had changed. He assessed the driver, who was in his mid-twenties, Caucasian, a bit overweight. Joe knew his back-up was nearby. He guessed they would be capable of responding to a change of plans. It seemed to him that Roy and his companion were just being cautious. After all, this was the first time Joe had bought from them. They had no more reason to trust him than he had to trust them. Roy said they would only be going a short distance, 'then we'll see the gear'. But then Joe had second thoughts. What if his back-up lost him en route to the new location? As a precaution, Joe was not carrying the $10,000 himself, but had entrusted it to a mate — one of his back-up team. For all he knew, Roy and his mate were planning to rip him off.

'No,' he told Roy. 'You go get it and come back. I'll be waiting.' Roy and Alex had a short conversation before Roy said to Alex, 'You go fetch it and we'll meet in the car park in the park.'

Roy got out of the Holden and transferred to Joe's car while Alex drove off. Joe sensed there was a tension between them. He tried to ease it by inviting Roy to count the money, even though he didn't have it. Roy shook his head. 'No, not now.' Joe knew he had been lucky. If Roy had said yes then he would have had to admit that his 'mate' was holding the cash. Joe had called Roy's bluff and got away with it. Roy repeated his earlier apology for all the 'stuffing around'.

'The gear has come from lots of different sources and not everyone wants to let go,' Roy explained. 'Especially that much gear at one time. I'll do the three hundred today and if everything is sweet all you have to do is give me a call and say, "Roy, it's Joe," and everything will be smooth.'

Joe reminded him of their agreement on cutting the price but in the meantime Roy had changed his mind. The price for future buys would be the same: $27 a bottle.

'Let's go,' said Roy. 'There's a park just down the road. I prefer to leave here [the McDonald's car park] anyway. You don't know who's who.'

As they drove along the highway towards the park Roy said, 'I don't want to do time. I've already done two years and I don't want to do any more.'

Joe sensed that Roy had calmed down.

'I'll have a look at the gear,' he said, 'then we'll go back to Macca's because my mate has got the money.'

Roy looked surprised but didn't seem to realise his bluff had been called earlier. 'You should have told me,' he said. 'I just don't like prearranged spots.'

He directed Joe to a car park at the corner of Beryl Street and the Pacific Highway. Roy made a call on his mobile phone. A couple of minutes later Joe watched Alex drive past in the Holden. Roy got out of Joe's car and started to walk towards Alex, who had parked some distance away. Roy and Alex stood about ten metres from Joe's car and had a conversation. After a while, Joe approached them and pointed to a white box and plastic carry bag Alex was holding. 'What's going on?' he asked. 'Is this the gear?'

'Yes,' said Roy, taking the plastic bag while Alex opened the white box.

The box was full of 10 ml vials of steroids. Joe had a look at some of the vials. Then Roy opened the plastic carry bag and took out a 50 ml bottle for Joe to inspect. As they spoke, plainclothes police approached. Alex dropped the box of steroids and Roy dropped the plastic carry bag. They realised they had been set up. They bolted but were chased by the police and arrested in the park.

Roy was charged with supplying steroids and possessing steroids and cannabis. Alex was charged with supplying steroids. Both were eventually convicted of drug offences.

Coffs Harbour had been a textbook job. Even so, Joe had had to improvise when the circumstances changed. This time he'd got away with it. The potential risks of leaving his back-up had come to nothing. The subjects had been arrested and convicted and no one had got hurt. But things wouldn't always turn out so well.

Chapter 3

The Lebanese connection

In mid-1996 Joe was given a briefing on two new targets, Victor and Ronnie, who were trying to sell large quantities of stolen mobile phones. The mobiles were believed to be part of a $400,000 heist from an electronics warehouse in Sydney's eastern suburbs.

Ronnie and Victor, both in their early twenties, were Lebanese. They were not major thieves but middlemen always on the lookout for stolen property. Business had brought them into contact with some much bigger players. With luck Ronnie and Victor could lead police up the ladder to some big-time criminals and to the syndicates involved in the sale of goods stolen in major thefts.

Joe was given a dossier on Ronnie and Victor and told to arrange an introduction. The question, as always, was how? The dossier told Joe that they were careless—they were happy to deal with anyone who offered the chance of a quick dollar. Victor was the smarter of the two, and Joe judged him to be the best starting point. His phone number was in the dossier.

Joe dialled the number but Victor didn't answer, so Joe left a short message asking him to call back. Within minutes Joe's phone was ringing. It was Victor. As soon as they had introduced themselves Joe asked, 'How are you, brother? I was told that you can help me out with some twenty-one tens [mobile phones].'

As expected, Victor jumped at the proposal. 'Yeah, mate. How many do you want?'

'That depends. If the price is right, I could take the whole lot.'

Victor said that someone else was holding the mobiles. He agreed to make some inquiries and ring back.

Joe put the phone down. It all sounded a bit too easy. Victor hadn't even bothered to ask how Joe had got his number. He was careless, but surely not this careless.

A few hours later Joe's phone rang. 'Hello?'

A male voice asked: 'Who's this?'

'Who's speaking?'

'Is it Joe?'

35

'Yeah. Who's that?'

'Ronnie.' It was Victor's partner.

'How are you, bro?' Joe asked.

'How do you know Victor?'

'Through you, you gave me his number.'

'How do you know me?'

'I've met you before.'

Ronnie sounded confused. 'You know me?'

'Yeah. You're Lebanese, right?'

'Yeah,' said a seemingly satisfied Ronnie.

The conversation turned to the purchase of the stolen mobile phones. Ronnie was as eager as Victor to arrange a deal.

Over the next couple of weeks Joe, Ronnie and Victor spoke about the deal and what they could do for one another. Ronnie and Victor claimed to have access to five hundred stolen Nokias and several hundred stolen Ericssons. They were offering a hundred of the Nokias for $410 each but wouldn't put a price on the Ericssons. Joe put in an order for five hundred Nokias.

At this point Ronnie and Victor finally showed some caution. They didn't want to let go of all the phones at once. They suggested Joe buy a hundred phones a day over five days. Ronnie and Victor had finally twigged to the possibility the deal could be a police sting or even a rip-off by other crooks. They knew that neither the cops nor other crooks would risk losing daily outlays of $41,000 cash. At the same time, neither would want to make a hit on the first day and risk losing the remaining four hundred phones. Ronnie and Victor imagined they were covering themselves against either contingency.

As is often the case in undercover work, negotiations dragged on with both sides making excuses to avoid keeping appointments: Ronnie was in Brisbane, Joe was in Wollongong, the phones were being held by someone else, the cash was being held by someone else. Suspicion bred suspicion. The problem wasn't just Joe. Victor was attempting to double-cross Ronnie, negotiating behind his back to increase his share of the profits at Ronnie's expense.

By early July Joe and his handlers were becoming increasingly frustrated and suspicious. There was a change of strategy: an arrest and the seizure of 100 mobiles was better than no arrest and no seizures. A buy-bust would be made on the purchase of the first 100 Nokias. But once again Ronnie was not available and Victor wanted to put things off for a few days. 'No,' said Joe. 'No more delays. The deal happens now or never.' It was nearly a month since Joe had first made contact with Victor and Ronnie and the three still hadn't met. All their negotiations had been carried out over the phone. It was time for a meeting.

Victor offered 'ten Nokias today and the rest in a couple of days'. Joe accepted: at least some progress was being made. But Joe's handlers had had enough. For all Joe's efforts, there was still a chance they would come away with nothing. A decision was made over Joe's head: if the deal went through, they were going to arrest Victor.

On the afternoon of 9 July, Joe followed Victor's instructions to drive to the car park of the Stocklands Mall at Merrylands and wait for him. At last Joe thought he was getting somewhere.

After a short time Victor pulled alongside. He was driving a white van. There was an Asian man in the passenger seat whom Joe didn't know. The man stayed in the van and Victor made no effort to introduce them. Victor was about twenty years old, thin, Mediterranean-looking. He was wearing a shirt with a tie. According to Joe, 'He looked like a salesman.' The Asian man was the supplier of the phones. He had set the limit of the sale at ten phones, Victor said, because 'he doesn't trust you because he has never done business with you'.

Victor put the phones in the boot of Joe's car and Joe handed over the $4000 cash—$100 had been knocked off the price because of all the 'stuffing around'. Another ten phones were available later in the day, if Joe wanted them.

Before they could leave the car park all three were arrested by police. Like the two targets, Joe was handcuffed and placed in a separate police vehicle. Once away from the scene he was released. Mock arrests like this—intended to protect an undercover cop for future operations or to extend a covert operation to enable other arrests to be made—don't always work. In cases where the target realises they have been set up, the operative's cover is immediately blown. If a target pleads not guilty then the undercover cop almost always has to give evidence at the court. However, in cases where a target pleads guilty, the cover can be maintained with the story that the operative has been dealt with at another court or has bribed the police to let him go. Unfortunately for Joe, Victor guessed straightaway that he'd been set up. Within hours Victor was on the phone. Continuing his role-playing, Joe congratulated Victor on getting bail. But it was no use: Victor knew the truth. 'Joe, they tell me you're an undercover cop. How could you? Why didn't you warn me? You're one of us.'

During their attempts to get a confession from Victor the arresting police had blown Joe's cover—but no one had thought to warn him.

A few days later Joe got a call from Ronnie. He was furious and threatening. 'You know you fucked up big time, cuz. Why did you do it? We're all Lebanese, fuck you. You should be worried.'

In the following days other calls gave Joe the same message: 'Watch your back. We'll get you. We'll find out where you live.'

Joe was stunned. He couldn't believe they had rung and threatened him, knowing that he was an undercover cop. He didn't fear them personally—he knew from police records and from briefings by his handlers that Ronnie and Victor were not the violent type—but he was worried that they might identify him to others who would have no qualms about harming him. Above all, he was worried for his family. 'This sort of thing is always in the back of your mind; that someone will get back at you through your family. As an undercover cop you know how to protect yourself but you can't be there all the time to protect your family.'

If Joe was concerned, his supervisors were not. 'Forget it,' was their response. 'Nothing's going to happen.' They seemed to know something Joe didn't.

In the end nothing did happen. Ronnie and Victor were small operators who had almost as much to fear from each other as they had from Joe, if only they knew it. Ronnie had threatened Joe over the double-cross without realising that Victor had double-crossed him. It was only Victor's treachery in sidelining his partner from the deal that had saved Ronnie from arrest.

From a police point of view the sting had been a limited success. Arrests had been made and a few mobiles were recovered, but the operation had not taken them further up the ladder. The thieves who stole the phones from the warehouse had not been caught. While a few dozen were recovered in unrelated police operations, most were sold through shonky mobile phone outlets in Sydney and Melbourne.

*

There was always a list of outstanding jobs waiting for Joe. During his gym workouts Joe met 'Peter', a user of steroids and other drugs who worked as a bouncer for several Kings Cross nightclubs and did a bit of drug dealing. They talked about doing business. Peter mentioned Adam, a speed supplier who operated in the Georges Hall–Merrylands area in Sydney's south-west. Adam dealt in ounces, Pete said, but he could supply a pound on request. He was money hungry and always on the hunt for new customers: just the type of target Joe was looking for. Joe asked Pete for an introduction and Pete was happy to oblige, hoping there would be something in it for him—either cash or drugs.

On 21 June 1996 Peter and Joe met 35-year-old Adam Rechin at the Louise Pizzeria in the Plaza at Bass Hill. Sitting beside him was 30-year-old Allan Metin Omayoglue, known as Metin, Adam's protection. Both were Lebanese. Adam was the taller of the two at around 180 centimetres, clean shaven, thin and fit-looking. Metin was a bit shorter, overweight, with a trim goatee beard: a bodyguard but no athlete. They chatted over coffee but when the discussion drifted towards drugs Adam cut them short. 'Let's go back to my place,' he said. 'We can't talk here.'

Peter and Joe followed Adam and Metin to a house in Georges Hall. Inside, Adam produced a home-made bong and a small bag of cannabis. As they got settled, he started to smoke. No one else was offered a puff.

'Let's talk business,' he said at last. 'What do you want?' He claimed to be able to supply whatever quantity of speed Joe wanted. 'It's top quality,' he insisted. 'If you want one or two ounces you will have to pay up front. If you want more, like four and up, I can get them and you can pay when you pick it up.'

Adam and Joe went into another room to continue the conversation. Adam produced a set of electronic scales and some speed in a plastic bag. Joe weighed the speed: there was 29 grams in the bag. 'How much?' he asked.

'$1200.'

'I hope it's good.'

'It is.'

Joe had cash on him; you couldn't play the part of a drug dealer with empty pockets. He gave Adam the money. They agreed to meet again and Adam gave Joe his phone number. After leaving the house, Joe dropped Peter off.

A few hours later, Joe rang Adam and asked to buy some more. He knew it was good gear, he said, and he was going to have no trouble selling it. Adam told him to come on over.

Joe had hardly walked through the door when Adam started talking prices. His supplier had three ounces and wanted 'three two'.

'I was after a bit more than that,' said Joe.

'How much?'

'Half a pound.'

'Shouldn't be a problem. My supplier is getting a new batch next week. I can't tell you the price right now. If you want eight [ounces] I'll get you eight, but I expect you to take it all because I can't afford to pay for it.'

'I don't like fucking people around,' said Joe. 'I'll take the eight. You have my word.'

Adam was a very active dealer. Apart from selling speed and cannabis, he had also grown his own hydroponic crops. He showed the apparatus to Joe. 'Look at the ceiling. I had lights all around here. I grew one hundred and twenty plants at a time. You should have seen them. There were heads everywhere. My mate and I did it together. He put up the money and I lived here rent-free for three months and in the end we made sixty thousand dollars each. Not bad, eh? If you're interested I can set it up for you. I have all the equipment and you could look after them once or twice a week.'

'Thanks,' said Joe, 'but I'm more interested in the goey.' He reminded Adam that he hadn't given him a price for the half-pound.

Adam left the room to make a call. 'You're not going to like this. For half it's $7600.'

The price was higher than Joe was expecting. Adam waited for Joe to speak. Joe didn't say no but insisted on knowing the quality before he would agree to the price.

'That's cool,' said Adam. 'It's a new batch. Top quality.'

Over the next week there were several telephone calls and a couple of meetings where they discussed the deal. Adam refused to talk business on the phone.

Early on the evening of 27 June, Joe received a call. It was Adam. He asked Joe to come over straightaway. He wanted to close the deal. Joe arrived about 9 pm. The drugs weren't in the house, Adam told him. Someone was going to deliver them. That someone was Metin.

When Metin arrived, Adam took him into another room. They spoke for a while with the door shut before Adam emerged and gave Joe the eight ounces. Joe put the speed in the black leather suitcase he had brought with him. Together they walked to Joe's car which was parked outside the house. Joe opened the boot to show Adam the cash. It was the sign to waiting police that the deal had gone down. Adam and Joe were arrested. The eight ounces were seized. Cash and other drugs—ecstasy tablets, ten cannabis plants and cannabis leaf—were found inside the house. Adam was charged with supplying and possessing drugs, and cultivating cannabis. Metin was also charged.

Adam pleaded guilty to drug supply and, surprisingly, was given a term of periodic detention. He was also ordered to undergo drug and alcohol rehabilitation.

Metin was not so lucky. In 1993 he had been convicted of possessing cannabis plants and fined $3000. In 1999 he pleaded guilty to the three-year-old charges and was sentenced to three years and nine months in jail.

The operation had been a success. It followed earlier operations that had resulted in the arrest and jailing of several low to mid-level dealers. Adam's supplier, however, had got away. During Joe's conversations with Adam and Metin in the lead-up to Adam's arrest, it had always been Adam who did the talking. In addition to the speed and cannabis, Adam claimed to have a supplier 'who has thousands of the ones with Doves on them [ecstasy tablets]. He wants $26 each and I will give them to you for $27 each.' Asked how many tablets the supplier had, Adam replied, 'One thousand, two thousand, three thousand. How many do you want?'

Joe wanted to complete the speed deal first but said he was interested in an ecstasy sample. While Joe had been confident that the speed deal was going to work, he knew Adam was not telling him the whole truth. For a start, Adam refused to name his supplier and kept making mistakes in remembering the cover story he had told Joe. Adam had said that his supplier was a woman and at different times added bits of information about her, but on a few occasions he slipped up and referred to his supplier as being a man.

As they waited for the deal to happen Adam realised he was getting his story confused and admitted to Joe that 'she' was a 'he' and that he was supplying 'three to four pounds a week easy'.

Police believed the supplier to be Harry Lahood, a well-known crime figure and convicted drug importer. In 1988 Lahood had been sentenced to 24 years' jail for the importation of 420 kilograms of cannabis with a street value of more than $4.5 million. He was ordered to forfeit $180,000 under the Commonwealth proceeds of crime legislation. Lahood argued unsuccessfully that $130,000 should be deducted as that was the amount he used to bribe police.

He was released from jail in 1993, having served only five years of a 24-year sentence. It was a move that surprised many at the time: how does anyone get released after serving only 20 per cent of a sentence? In 1999 he was rearrested for supplying heroin and amphetamines but the charges were later dropped. Lahood was described at the Wood Royal Commission as a major heroin trafficker.

Whether or not Adam's supplier really was Harry Lahood, he had succeeded in slipping through the net, but there were plenty of big fish and it wouldn't be long before Joe was given the chance to go after another.

Chapter 4
Garry Page and 'Lawrie'

'Sam' was a longtime Kings Cross drug dealer. Joe socialised with him from time to time and they had done some small business deals together. Although not in his league, Sam was an associate of the notorious Kings Cross crime boss Louis Bayeh, whose involvement in drugs, police corruption and protection had attracted considerable attention at the Wood Royal Commission into the New South Wales Police Service. Several of Sam's relatives were also mentioned in connection with Bayeh.

About 7.30 pm on Wednesday 2 October 1996, Joe drove to Bayswater Road, Kings Cross, for a meeting with Sam. There was someone Sam wanted Joe to meet. They had a short conversation on the footpath before Sam called over a solid, fit-looking man in his fifties who had been standing nearby. He introduced the man as Garry.

Garry worked out regularly in a gym and trained in martial arts. His upper body was covered in tattoos. He looked every inch the Kings Cross tough guy. Although Joe didn't recognise him when they met, it wouldn't take him long to put a name to the stranger. Garry was Garry Page, an eastern suburbs crook who had done jail time for murder and was suspected of being the getaway driver in the 1992 shotgun murder of 56-year-old underworld figure and standover man Desmond 'Dessie' Anthony Lewis. In the same year Page beat charges of aiding and abetting and obtaining money by deception. In March 1996 the director of public prosecutions had decided not to proceed with charges against Page of conspiracy to rob while armed, robbery in company and impersonating a police officer. Page had pleaded guilty to one charge of assault with intent to commit a felony, but his sentence was deferred and he was fined $2000. Garry's networks extended to Michael Hurley, who was regarded by both crooks and police alike as a 'head honcho' of organised crime. (Hurley died in jail in 2007 while under remand on charges of conspiring to import cocaine.)

There was a short conversation before Garry said, 'There's no use fucking about. I'll take you straight to the man. He's a good bloke. I have known him since I was a kid.'

GARRY PAGE AND 'LAWRIE'

Joe was wary. He didn't know who he was going to meet, nor did he know much about Garry. But he knew how Sam operated and he knew that Sam would be eyeing a share of any deal that resulted from the introduction. Deciding that there was some safety in Sam's involvement, Joe agreed to go with Garry.

Garry got into Joe's car and directed him to the Bondi Beachside Inn, overlooking Bondi Beach. They went into the hotel and Garry took Joe to room 710, where 'the man' was waiting for them. His name was 'Lawrie'. Joe had never seen him before.

Like Garry, Lawrie was in his fifties. Unlike Garry, he never went near a gym. He was shabby and overweight. The room itself was a mess, with clothing strewn everywhere. Lawrie turned out to be an Australian citizen resident in the Philippines. Lawrie had been knocking around Sydney's underworld for a long time. He claimed to have 'worked' at the infamous illegal gambling club, the 33 Club in Goulburn Street, the nearby Associated Motor Club and South Sydney Juniors during the 1960s and early 1970s, when the Moffitt Royal Commission investigated and found evidence of the infiltration of organised crime—masterminded by McPherson, Freeman and others—in licensed clubs. For years afterwards Lawrie drifted around the club industry. He had been involved in the drug trade for several decades.

On his visits to Sydney, Lawrie dealt in drugs and anything else he could get his hands on, mostly in Bondi and the eastern suburbs, to cover the costs of his Australian holiday and to cash himself up before returning to the Philippines. At the time Joe met him, Lawrie was managing a bar in the Philippines. He'd just taken a beating over a mix-up with the protection money that had to be paid to local authorities and was back in Australia until things settled down.

'I want an ounce [of grass] to see how good it is,' said Joe. 'How much have you got all up?'

Walking over to the wardrobe, Lawrie pulled out a pound bag. 'About five pounds,' he said. 'The price is $18,000 for the lot.' He took some grass from the bag and measured an ounce on a set of electronic scales. 'I'll let you have this for $350.'

Joe had brought cash in expectation of a deal. He paid Lawrie for the ounce. Then Lawrie asked, 'Are you interested in speed?'

'I could be,' said Joe.

They discussed price, quality, the amount available and delivery time. Lawrie seemed happy at the prospect of doing business with Joe, but said he would have to make some inquiries. He warned Joe about the need for caution when using the phones and they came up with a code: one hour of water-skiing would be an ounce while a day on the boat would be one pound. Joe then offered to 'take the five [pounds of cannabis] off you next week, if you can hold them for me'. The deal agreed, Joe dropped Garry back at the Cross. For Joe it was a good day's work; the first buy had gone well and he appeared to have won Lawrie's and Garry's trust.

Over the next couple of days Joe and Lawrie spoke several times on the phone. As usual, each one put up an excuse as to why the next deal had to be delayed 'for a day or two'. Lawrie was buying time because he had not been able to obtain the drug but did not want to admit it. Joe was buying time to keep control of the situation: the deal was to be done on his terms, not Lawrie's. A week later Lawrie was trying to push Joe into buying at least a couple of the five pounds of grass he had as a show of good faith. He promised there was another eight pounds on the way. Joe could have first refusal on it, provided he took some of the grass Lawrie was holding now.

On the evening of 11 October Joe drove to Bondi to pick up Lawrie. After getting into the car Lawrie handed Joe a yellow plastic bag with a pound of grass inside. The deal looked okay and Joe handed over $3500. They looked forward to doing more business together.

Lawrie quickly forgot his own warnings about speaking on the phone. Over the next few weeks he became quite talkative. According to him, a friend of his in Adelaide had several pounds of speed and quite a bit of coke for sale. Some hash was also due from Thailand but it was still a few days away. It was coming in through Brisbane.

As Lawrie pressed Joe for another deal, Joe stuck to the script, wanting to see and test samples before he committed himself to large amounts. Joe's cover story was that he did not use drugs himself—he was in the business for profit—but he had a 'pilot', a user who would try the drugs and assess their quality. In fact, police used their drug test kits to assess the drugs or they were tested at the Drug Analytical Laboratories at Lidcombe. Experience and training had already made Joe something of an expert. When they were in powdered form he could make a preliminary assessment of their quality by smelling the drugs and looking at their texture, colour and consistency.

As well as drugs, Lawrie claimed to be able to get his hands on a wide variety of weapons ranging from handguns, including Beretta pistols and .357 calibre pistols, to machine pistols and sub-machine guns. 'We can get just about anything,' he boasted, 'And I mean anything.'

Like most traffickers, Lawrie knew that guns and drugs went hand in hand. Few traffickers have not been ripped off, bashed or shot at in the course of doing deals, or in revenge for ripping off someone else.

For the next couple of weeks Lawrie proved difficult to contact. Joe was worried. In fact, Lawrie had been in Queensland. A couple of times, when calling Lawrie, Joe found himself talking instead to one of Lawrie's offsiders, a man who called himself Fred. Sometimes Fred suggested to Joe that the two of them might be able to do business.

On 27 November Fred called Joe to suggest a meeting. Lawrie, he said, was 'not available'.

'What are you going to be wearing?' asked Joe.

'Grey pants and a blue jacket.'

'I'll be driving a dark coloured Mazda.'

That evening Joe drove to the corner of Alison Road and Cook Street, Randwick. When he pulled up, Fred jumped in the car. Fred was a short man in his forties, slender with thinning hair. 'He looked,' Joe recalled later, 'like a retired jockey, fidgety and up to no good.'

'I've just spoken to Lawrie,' Fred told him. 'He wants me to let you know that he has a machine gun pistol for sale, plus thirty rounds of ammunition. When you take off the stock it becomes a pistol.'

'How much?' asked Joe.

'He wants four thousand,' said Fred. 'I told him it was too much but he reckoned it was a fair price because the gun is clean.'

'Where is it from?'

'The Australian army.'

They laughed. 'I guess that means it works,' said Joe. 'But I'll have to have a look at it first.'

'There's some jewellery,' said Fred. 'Are you interested?'

'What are we talking about?'

'Lawrie has a gold necklace with four diamonds in it, with a matching bracelet. It was bought overseas for about eight thousand US which makes it worth about ten thousand here. Lawrie reckons he'll let you have it for four.'

'Not really my line,' said Joe.

'What about fake credit cards? Fifteen hundred each. As many as you want.'

Joe told Fred he was interested in the gun but said no to the rest. The more Joe was offered, the more he wondered whether it was a test. Fred might be thinking that an over-enthusiastic undercover cop would take anything on offer, just for the pinch. The conversation ended with Fred telling Joe to give Lawrie a call. The relationship between Lawrie and Fred was unclear. Lawrie had already mentioned guns to him. As for the rest—the jewellery and fake credit cards—Joe couldn't be sure whether Fred was acting as go-between for Lawrie or was in it for himself.

The next day Joe rang Lawrie and they arranged to meet that night. Lawrie was now minding a friend's unit in Tunbridge Street, Botany. He knew about the meeting with Fred and what had been discussed. Joe arrived with plenty of cash. They sat down at the dining table and Lawrie pulled a small plastic resealable bag out of his pocket and handed it to Joe. It was a sample of cocaine. Lawrie had an ounce lined up, if Joe was interested. He also offered Joe the gold necklace with diamonds and matching bracelet for sale as a set for $5500. Joe repeated that he wasn't interested, while noting that the price was $1500 more than Fred had quoted.

Lawrie stood up and went into one of the two bedrooms in the unit. A few moments later he came out carrying a green canvas bag. He put the bag on the table and opened it. Inside the bag were a black machine gun broken into several parts, a black magazine and some ammunition. Lawrie put the gun together and handed it to Joe. 'You can have it for $5500,' he said. 'And I'll throw in a banana clip [a curved ammunition clip].'

'It's too much,' said Joe. 'Freddy said the price was four thousand.'

'Bullshit he did.'

Joe shrugged. 'He told me four thousand.'

'That's not right, I'll ring Freddy.'

Lawrie rang Fred. After a short conversation he put Joe on the phone. 'The asking price was $5500,' said Fred, 'but I think we can do it for $4000.'

After putting the phone down Lawrie brought two one-pound bags of cannabis out of the bedroom and handed them to Joe: 'It's from Adelaide.' After inspecting it, Joe put the cannabis in the green bag on the table.

'You remember the hash I told you about?' said Lawrie. 'There's about 20 kilos coming in [through Brisbane] and

I've asked for five to eight pounds for myself. And there's ten thousand E's [ecstasy tablets] due in from Europe. You can have them for $22 a tablet.'

'What about the speed?' Joe asked.

'It's coming. I'll have it and the coke tomorrow. The E's will be here next week.'

Joe stuck to the routine he'd used before. 'I'll need samples,' he said. 'Get me some E's, speed and coke and let's see how we go.'

Meanwhile Lawrie stripped down the gun and put it in the bag with the drugs. He wanted $12,900 for the gun and the two pounds of cannabis from Adelaide. In light of his conversation with Fred, Joe made a counter offer: 'I'll give you $10,900 but I've only got $10,000 on me, so I'll have to owe you $900.'

Reluctantly, Lawrie agreed. The cash was in the boot of Joe's car. Joe picked up the canvas bag and walked with Lawrie to the car. He put the bag containing the gun and drugs on the back seat, then opened the boot and got out a plastic shopping bag containing $10,000 cash. He gave the money to Lawrie.

A week later Joe went to see Lawrie at the Tunbridge Street unit. This time there was a stranger there. About forty, with a battered face and a beer gut bulging over his trousers, Johno looked like an ex-footballer who'd long ago quit training. 'Johno is a mate,' said Lawrie. 'You can say anything in front of him. If I'm overseas you can deal with Johno.'

After handing Lawrie the $900 he owed from their last deal, Joe was given free samples of coke and speed—Lawrie had about half a pound of speed. It was Johno who was in contact with the ecstasy and speed suppliers. He vouched for the quality of the speed: 'It's local and I've sold it to the bikies with no problems.' Supply, he added, was not a worry.

Joe left Lawrie and Johno and, as usual, after making sure he was not being followed, went to meet his handlers. They discussed the next move. They knew Lawrie had other drugs in the apartment, but not what they were or how much. They considered—and rejected—a quick raid. By now they had enough on Lawrie: whether they arrested him now or later, he was going to do significant jail time. The truth was, another tantalising target had emerged: Garry.

Since meeting Garry, Joe had introduced him to another undercover operative. Garry was now expecting a large shipment of firearms from an outlaw bikie gang in Adelaide. He was also offering heroin for sale and had supplied an ounce to the other undercover operative. The decision was made to stall Lawrie on any further deals; if they arrested him it would alert Garry. While Joe would have preferred to go after Lawrie straightaway, he understood that it was important to get guns off the streets. But catching Garry was going to be harder than anyone imagined.

On 11 December Lawrie rang Joe and told him that the next buy was available, but Joe put him off.

'Mate, I'm not going to be able to take it.'

'What's that supposed to mean?'

'I'm sorry, mate. Something's come up. I can't take the stuff right now.'

'Mate, that's not how we do business. You told me you were rapt in the stuff and now you tell me that you don't want it. I have been holding this for five days and now you tell me that you don't fucking want it. I'm not making a cent on this. If you don't take it I'll look like an idiot. I lose face. Then my guy loses face with his mate who's supplying him. It's bad for all of us.'

Joe repeated his apology. Then he ran through a list of excuses: other deals he had in the offing, mates who owed him money, even a seriously ill father in Lebanon who needed money for an operation. But Lawrie was in no mood to listen to excuses. Before hanging up he said, 'You know this has fucked future business between us.'

Although contact between Lawrie and Joe continued until March the following year, there were no more deals: the sting was over. The police were chasing a bigger prize: the shipment of guns. Before they could move on Lawrie, he skipped the country.

Lawrie went back to running his clubs in the Philippines, having made a nice profit from his stay in Australia. The police still had Garry in their sights, but then disaster struck. Garry found a police listening device hidden in his apartment. There were suggestions, but no proof, that he had been tipped off by corrupt police. The shipment of guns was cancelled, at least until the suppliers and buyers had satisfied themselves that they were safe. But Garry was not as lucky as Lawrie. Garry had sold several handguns to the undercover cop he had been introduced to by Joe. In July 2000 Garry was convicted at the Sydney District Court of three charges of supplying drugs and one charge of supplying a firearm and sentenced to three and a half years' jail.

Joe was frustrated and angry at having put himself at risk to obtain evidence against Lawrie only to see him escape arrest. He resented even more the fact that there had been no major seizure of weapons. Nevertheless, Joe knew that disappointments like this were part of the job. Some cases you won and some you lost; even victory could be pyrrhic.

In the often paranoid world of undercover cops and criminals the failure of an operation always brings suspicion: of treachery or incompetence or indiscretion. It is all too easy to blame the person on the front line. When a sting goes wrong a question will always be left hanging in the air: 'Can he be trusted next time?'

Joe understood the personal dangers and the risks to his reputation, but all he could do was get on with the next job. As for Fred, Lawrie's would-be go-between, police couldn't lay a finger on him. Joe didn't hear of him again until several years later. Fred was still running around Sydney's eastern suburbs doing deals when he got the chance and staying out of trouble with the police.

Chapter 5

Garry Raff and John Visser

While infiltrating Lawrie's network, Joe was also buying amphetamines from Rob, a petty drug dealer and user in Wollongong. As usual, Joe's real interest in dealing with a small operator like Rob was to get passed up the line to the bigger suppliers. That meant asking Rob for larger amounts than he normally handled. He needed the extra drugs, he told Rob, to satisfy the demands of the people he supplied. Rob suggested Garry Raff, who lived at Summer Hill in Sydney's inner west. According to Rob, Raff moved large quantities of speed as well as pot from South Australia, which he sold for $3600 a pound. Rob rang him and told Raff to expect a call from Joe.

On 6 January 1997 Joe rang Raff and introduced himself as Rob's mate. Raff was circumspect but agreed to a meeting the next day at the Covent Garden Hotel in Sydney's Chinatown.

Raff was in his fifties, thin with cropped brown hair. Joe could tell at once that he was nervous.

'Mate,' said Raff, 'meeting strangers straight off is very risky so let's go for a walk to Darling Harbour.'

Once they started walking his nervousness dissipated. Before long he and Joe were discussing prices and amounts. Raff explained that an ounce of speed (or 'goey') would cost $4000. Told that the price was too high, Raff insisted it was top quality.

'My guy pays forty [thousand dollars] a pound. He will add ten straight on top. For that kind of money I want to make a few thousand. So for a pound you're looking at fifty-three [thousand dollars] minimum.'

Joe still said it was too much.

'In that case, mate, I don't know what I can do for you.'

'What's the best price you can give me?' asked Joe.

Raff wasn't happy but promised to make some inquiries. 'Meantime, mate, I can get coke if you're interested. Four thousand an ounce.'

'Sure,' said Joe. 'I'm interested.'

Suddenly Raff stopped walking. 'You haven't got anything on you, have you? You're a fit-looking bloke. You would get into the police force no trouble. Lift up your shirt.'

As Joe lifted his shirt and turned around, Raff patted him down for a wire [a listening device]. They were standing in front of Jordons Seafood Restaurant, near the Entertainment Centre—a place usually busy with tourists and businesspeople. A few passers-by watched and wondered what was going on.

Wearing a wire was always a risk. You could never be sure that a nervous target would not frisk you. But the chances of that happening were less once you had started doing business. Joe never wore a wire to a first meeting.

'Happy?' asked Joe.

'Nothing personal, mate. I had to make sure.'

Raff agreed to ring Joe in the next few days to talk about prices and availability. Afterwards they walked back towards the Covent Garden Hotel, over the years a favourite watering hole for some of Sydney's most notorious crooks. Its best known regulars were former detective Roger Rogerson and his criminal mates, Arthur 'Neddy' Smith and Graham 'Abo' Henry. During the 1980s, when Rogerson gave Smith and Henry the 'green light' to commit armed robberies in return for information and 'assistance' when required, Smith would often start the day with a beer at the Covent Garden Hotel. In his autobiography, *Neddy*, Smith described Rogerson 'taking his gear off and dancing on the tables'. As things turned out, the Covent Garden was one of the last hotels to serve Neddy Smith a drink. On 30 October 1987, after a day-long pub crawl that began at the Covent Garden, Smith was involved in a minor traffic dispute that ended with Smith stabbing Ronald Flavell, an innocent passenger in the other car. Smith was convicted of Flavell's murder and sentenced to spend the rest of his life in jail.

'The Covent Garden Hotel had a colourful past,' Joe recalls. 'Raff was obviously in his element. When a criminal suggests a meeting place you always get it checked out beforehand to make sure it's safe, so I had a pretty good idea of the clientele. Raff had been a bit jumpy when we met but he soon settled down. When we shook hands to leave, I was confident of hearing from him again.'

Six days later Joe met Raff in the main bar of the Summer Hill Hotel. After a couple of drinks they left the hotel, got into Joe's car and drove to Fleet Street near the railway station. Raff made a call on his mobile and left the car, telling Joe to wait. A few moments later Raff returned and handed Joe an ounce of speed, for which Joe paid him $4000. (Raff had been telling the truth about its quality: when tested, the speed would be found to be 74 per cent pure.) While they did the deal Joe noticed a blond-haired man lurking near the car. He didn't say anything to Raff but it wouldn't be long before Joe saw him again.

Meanwhile Raff told Joe that he had ten pounds of high-grade speed available for sale at $55,000 a pound. He also had access to a large amount of ecstasy tablets for between

GARRY RAFF AND JOHN VISSER

$23 and $25 each by the thousand, or $30 each by the hundred. Joe said he would buy a pound of speed. Two days later, at the same hotel, they sealed the deal.

About 7 pm on 16 January Joe met Raff in the Summer Hill car park near the railway station, but Raff now wanted to change the arrangements. He wanted to split the deal into two half-pound transactions rather than one for a pound. Joe agreed, knowing it would look suspicious if he objected. Raff left Joe and returned to the car a few minutes later with the half-pound of speed.

Looking in the rear-view mirror, Joe noticed the same blond-haired man he had seen loitering when they did their last deal. Joe guessed he was there for protection: to watch Raff's back and keep an eye out for police surveillance. When Raff left the car to pick up the speed, the lookout followed him. When Raff returned, so did he.

Joe and Raff got out of the car and went to the boot to get the cash. As Joe handed the money over, heavily armed members of the State Protection Group pounced. Joe was 'arrested' along with Raff. The lookout ran, but after a short chase and struggle he was overpowered and arrested. He was in his mid-forties, fit and muscular, with tattoos on his forearms. His name was John Visser and he was Raff's supplier.

Raff and Visser faced a series of charges for supplying and possessing drugs. Their application for bail was initially refused but since there was little evidence against Visser he was bailed at a later hearing.

Within days Joe received a call from his supervisor. Information had been received that Raff and Visser had a contract hit out on the 'Crown witness against them'. Joe was the only Crown witness. The hitman, whose identity was not known, would be given a handgun for the job and paid $100,000, made up of a half-pound of speed and $50,000 cash.

Joe was told to 'lie low' for the next few days while the police gathered more information. He was worried and was right to be. As well as being a well-documented drug user and dealer, Raff had a record of violence. On 22 May 1985, Raff was running along New Brighton Beach, near Lismore, when his leg became entangled in the fishing line of 25-year-old Dale Toovey. An argument followed and Raff drew a knife and stabbed Toovey. He then made Toovey walk into the surf to drown. Raff was charged with murder. Found not guilty by a jury on the grounds of mental illness—the court heard Raff was suffering chronic paranoid schizophrenia—the presiding Justice directed that Raff 'be kept in strict custody until the Governor's pleasure be known'. He was released from jail in 1994. Joe had known of Raff's record and reputation during the operation but nobody told him about John Visser until after Visser was arrested. Had he known about him earlier, Joe might have had second thoughts about the job.

Visser was a career criminal with a history of extreme violence. He had been sentenced to life imprisonment for the 1982 gelignite bombing of a car driven by a partner, Gerard Flaherty, but would serve just over a decade before being released. Flaherty's two young children were in the car when it exploded. All three survived the bombing, but they were seriously injured: Flaherty lost a leg and one of his children lost the sight of one eye.

Visser and Flaherty had been partners in a car-stealing racket and Visser didn't appreciate being told that it was over. But there was more to it than business: Visser had discovered that Flaherty was having an affair with his wife and for that he was determined to kill him. At his capture Visser had pulled a gun and threatened to shoot police, but he was eventually overpowered and arrested.

In the late 1980s police allege that one of the detectives involved in Visser's 1982 arrest was the target of a $100,000 hit. Not long after the contract was issued, the detective's private car was sprayed with bullets while parked in the driveway of his western suburbs home. A month later his car was firebombed. Visser has not been charged over either incident. The former detective described Visser as being 'totally mad and ruthless. He keeps a grudge forever. Violence means nothing to him.'

Seven years after his arrest, Visser appeared as a witness for Tom Domican when Domican faced his trial over conspiring to murder Superintendent Ronald Woodham, the then head of the Internal Investigation Unit at Long Bay jail and later head of the Corrective Services Department. When Visser gave evidence, the Crown prosecutor, Mr Chris Maxwell, put to him that he had a 'hit list' of police who had been involved in his 1982 arrest. Visser denied the allegation, saying 'It's the first I've heard of it.' At the time, Domican was regarded as one of Sydney's most dangerous criminals. (In 1997 Joe was assigned to target Domican. See Chapter 7.)

In 1997 Raff pleaded guilty to several drug supply charges and was sentenced to a minimum of six years' jail. It was not until August 2001 that the charges against Visser were finalised but when the case went to trial he was acquitted.

On 3 April 2007 the then 56-year-old Visser was arrested again. Two days later he appeared before the Central Local Court where he was refused bail on a series of supply and possession charges relating to heroin, methylamphetamine and MDMA (ecstasy) tablets. Placed in a holding cell with another man who had been allowed bail for a separate offence, Visser grabbed the opportunity when his cellmate fell asleep and a Corrective Services officer asked which of them had been granted bail. Visser answered, gave the other prisoner's name, signed the bail papers and walked out of the building. Within weeks he was on the New South Wales Police's '10 Most Wanted', list. Joe learned of Visser's escape by chance when he was looking through the most wanted list some months after the escape.

Visser left the country and remained on the run until 14 May 2008 when he was arrested at Melbourne airport after flying in from Amsterdam. He was extradited to Sydney and on 6 March 2009 pleaded guilty to six charges of supplying drugs, three counts of possessing drugs and escaping from lawful custody. One year later Visser was sentenced to a total of seven years and eight months' jail.

Chapter 6
The finished article

Among the undercover operations assigned to Joe, one was personal—the killing of another cop. On 17 April 1997, 25-year-old Constable David Carty of Fairfield police finished his shift at midnight and went out with other off-duty police to have a drink at the local Cambridge Tavern. As he was leaving the tavern in the early hours he was attacked by a group of men and stabbed in the chest, kicked and stomped on. Carty died as a result of the injuries.

A group of youths known as the Assyrian Kings was believed to be responsible for killing Constable Carty. Joe, along with other undercover police, was given the job of working on them. They were not to infiltrate the group but to watch them closely in order to identify members and their associates, and record their movements.

At the end of the operation a number of people were charged. Gilbert Adam was convicted of the murder and sentenced to twenty-eight years' jail. His brother, Richard, beat all charges. Edward Esho and Thaier Sako were jailed for six years and eight months and five years respectively for inflicting grievous bodily harm on Carty. Three others, Amier Yaco, James George and Eshmail Esha, were acquitted of all charges relating to the attack.

Carty lost his life because he had 'chipped' (rebuked) Esho over his behaviour in the tavern earlier in the evening. Investigating the murder took a heavy toll on his colleagues. Joe and Carty were friends; they had worked together at Fairfield. Jobs like this were not part of the training, for detectives or undercover police.

In September 1997 Joe was given another target, Michael Mann. Originally from Serbia, Mann was a longtime Melbourne criminal who several years earlier had changed his name by deed poll from Miroslav Milenkovic. During the early 1990s Mann had turned up in Double Bay, in Sydney's eastern suburbs, claiming to be a wealthy architect. Lunching and dining every day at expensive restaurants, he soon made himself known among the rich Double Bay set. He was particularly interested in befriending Jewish families and jewellers.

One day Mann became the talk of Double Bay when he walked into a car showroom and bought a red 348 Ferrari sports car, paying for it with $140,000 in cash which he was carrying in a David Jones shopping bag. He told the salesman, 'I won it at the races.' He later sold the Ferrari and bought a British racing green Bentley Turbo sedan.

Mann also bought plenty of jewellery, including a gold Rolex watch, which he asked the jeweller to 'do up' by adding a number of diamonds to its face. Meanwhile he came to the attention of local police because of his association with another group in the eastern suburbs: a gang of Serbian drug traffickers and violent criminals headed by Milivoje 'Skinny Mischa' Matovic and his lieutenant, who was known simply as 'The Eyebrow' because he had one dark and one blonde eyebrow.

Mann and Skinny Mischa had plenty in common: they both loved the high life but weren't interested in the sort of honest work that would pay for it. But Skinny Mischa and his gang weren't exactly thrilled at Mann's behaviour since arriving on the scene. Mann's antics, especially his habit of throwing money around, drew attention to himself—and, therefore, to them. Meanwhile Mann expanded his social circle by teaming up with another gang of criminals led by the well-known underworld figure Robert Douglas 'Bertie' Kidd, whose specialities were large robberies and violence.

With these connections it was not surprising that police soon suspected Mann of being involved in a series of violent home invasions and the theft of cash and jewellery from expensive homes across Sydney's eastern suburbs and lower north shore. It turned out that most of the victims knew Mann.

By late August 1997 the police had enough evidence to charge Mann with a home invasion at Drummoyne where a 9.15 carat diamond and other jewellery were stolen and their elderly female owner bashed. By then detectives had learned that Mann was wanted in Victoria in connection with a home invasion committed several years earlier. Victorian police were told of his arrest but Mann was released on bail before any decision could be made to extradite him. Frustrated Sydney police decided to mount another operation against him. The job was given to Joe.

Joe's introduction to Mann was arranged by an unsuspecting Double Bay criminal he had befriended earlier. The cover story was that Joe was attempting to arrange a false passport for a criminal in jail on remand for armed hold-ups. In early September Joe rang Mann, who appeared to be expecting the call. A meeting was agreed and Mann told Joe, 'I'll meet you upstairs at the Sheraton on the Park in an hour. I'll be wearing a blue suit and blue tie.' The suddenness of the meeting was deliberate. It put Mann in control. If Joe was a cop, it gave him little time to get set up.

Mann was in the coffee shop when Joe arrived. He was a well-built man in his thirties with a barrel chest and fine facial features. Mann was well spoken but Joe noticed a hint of his old Serbian accent. They discussed a common 'friend' who had appeared before the court earlier that day. Told by Joe that the friend had been refused bail, Michael replied, 'All he can do now is go for Supreme Court bail which he'll more than likely get. If he can get bail, I told him that I can get him a passport.'

'Yeah, he told me,' said Joe. 'That's why I'm here.'

'So you said.'

'Can you help?'

'Maybe. The truth is, mate, I'm a bit paranoid at the moment. I have a few problems.'

'Nothing serious, I hope.'

'I'll be up front with you,' said Mann. 'It's not going to be cheap. We get a legit passport from someone and we pay them $5000. We then take the passport to someone in Immigration who fixes the entry date and he gets $3000. Then the guy who changes the photo gets $1000 and I get another $1000. All I need from you is four colour photos and the money up front. It will take ten to fourteen working days.'

'That sounds good to me,' said Joe. 'I'll pass it on. Of course it depends on whether he gets bail. If he gets knocked back then I don't suppose my guy will be needing a passport.'

They laughed, and Mann began to open up on his own problems. 'The police are going around telling everybody that I'm an armed robber. There was a jewellery shop in Double

Bay that was held up and two or three million dollars' worth of stock taken. The police think I'm behind it. I don't need this shit.'

'Who does?' Joe chipped in.

'Not your problem, though, is it?' said Mann. 'If there's anything else your mate wants, tell him I can get my hands on fake birth certificates and interstate driver's licences for $1000 each.'

Before Joe could answer, Mann's phone rang. After speaking to the caller he told Joe he had to go.

During the next four weeks Joe had several meetings with Mann, as well as frequent telephone conversations. Mann confided in Joe that he was wanted in Melbourne for a $100,000 home invasion: '[A]bout five years ago I got to know this Asian bloke. I knew the set-up of his house, so I organised these five guys to do the place over. The family had a heap of antiques. I got charged. When they gave me bail I pissed off.'

Mann admitted to spending a total of more than six years in jail in Melbourne for stealing. He also spoke of a friend in Sydney whom he called 'Mad Max'. Mad Max was later identified as an erratic, heroin-using, pistol-wielding criminal believed responsible for a number of violent robberies and home invasions.

Mann raised the prospect of doing a home invasion with Joe in Melbourne worth 'at least $100,000'. Mann had already lined up a third person, and guns had been arranged. Mann also spoke about a possible kidnapping which would involve holding a husband and wife for a multi-million dollar ransom. The target was a wealthy Jewish family that lived in Rose Bay. Michael was convinced the family would not report the kidnapping to police as the husband was involved in some shady deals and had a lot of cash and jewellery which would be difficult to explain to police and the Tax Office. But the kidnapping was on hold, Mann said, until he knew whether he was going to be jailed for the antiques robbery.

As the meetings continued, Mann told Joe that, before his arrest in Melbourne, he had been approached by a businessman who claimed to be representing police and who told Mann that for $30,000 the charges against him could be made to disappear. Mann said he refused the offer and was charged.

Joe had heard a lot of talk about Mann around the eastern suburbs. Mann was a larger than life figure and Joe wondered whether the supposed 'bribe' was not simply a scam by the businessman. Mann said he had similar doubts and that was why he rejected the offer. Later, however, Mann told Joe about another attempted bribe, and this time Joe was not so sure that it was a scam. According to Mann, 'Detective [name given] has it in for me and wants $10,000 for the Victorian extradition papers to go away.' Again, Mann claimed to have rejected the offer, this time because he was not satisfied the detective could deliver on the deal. The reason the detective 'has it in for me', Mann said, was because he had 'stolen' the wife of a friend of the detective. The woman had left her husband, a wealthy eastern suburbs businessman, and was now married to Mann.

Joe had plenty of reasons for believing Mann's story about the attempted 'bribes'—even if they were scams. After all, Mann gave every appearance of being rich and successful. He lived in a fancy apartment overlooking the harbour in Sydney's Edgecliff, always had wads of cash in his pockets, drove luxury cars and wore Versace clothes. He seemed to be just the type of criminal a corrupt police officer or opportunistic crook might want to shake down. At the same time, Joe knew that Mann was a conman and liar. For all he knew, Mann was making it all up. Nevertheless, he reported the conversation to his supervisor.

About a week later the operation was abruptly terminated. Mann was due back in court and the opportunity to gather evidence about other home invasions Mann had organised, as well as about the bandits themselves, had passed.

What Joe didn't know was that Mann was in severe financial trouble. His extravagant spending far outstripped his share of the robberies he planned. To make matters worse, his wife was not as wealthy as he had believed; Mrs Mann could not keep him in the lifestyle he wanted.

The operation and the way it ended were a disappointment for Joe. Despite all Mann's lies and exaggerations, Joe knew he would have been a prize scalp. He was not like the drug traffickers Joe was used to dealing with, with their code words and their secret meeting places and their endless haggling over amounts and prices. Mann was flash, full of himself, and garrulous. But to get anything really valuable out of him would take time. Mann was only too happy to talk about future robberies, but that wasn't what Joe wanted to hear. What he was after was information about home invasions already committed, including the names of Mann's partners. In wrapping up the operation, Joe's superiors had thrown away his chance of luring Mann into making a mistake. It was another important lesson for Joe: however much he might work alone, as an undercover cop he would never be his own boss.

Mann's story did not end there. His most dangerous enemy was himself, not Joe. The Victoria Police did not proceed with his extradition to Melbourne and in December 1997, after Joe had moved on to another job in another squad, Mann was charged in Sydney with robbery while armed with a dangerous weapon and receiving stolen property. Two and a half years later he was sentenced to five years' jail.

Paroled in August 2002, Mann was arrested a year later in Melbourne and again charged with armed robbery. In March 2004, while still on bail, Mann and two others committed another robbery on a home in Melbourne.

He was eventually sentenced to seven years' jail for the 2003 robbery and a total of eleven years' jail for the 2004 robbery and a related offence. Mann's victims had not changed since Mann's first conversations with Joe: most were wealthy old ladies living in the affluent suburbs of Sydney and Melbourne. In a final twist Mann's wife, perhaps realising why he was attracted to her in the first place, divorced him.

Mann's Sydney associates did not fare any better. The bashed victim of one of the home invasions that Mann was believed to have organised told detectives that the robber 'looked like the actor in *Who Framed Roger Rabbit?*' The short, balding actor was Bob Hoskins and there was only one crook the victim could have been describing: Bertie Kidd.

In another robbery believed to have been set up by Mann, thieves entered a Kings Cross jewellery shop through the roof and hid there until the shop was opened in the morning. The thieves then crashed through the ceiling, tied up the owner and assistant, and stole an estimated several million dollars' worth of jewellery. When detectives arrived, Kidd was seen sitting in the coffee shop opposite, calmly sipping his coffee as he watched the investigation.

In December 1997 police raided the Waverley home of Eric Leonard Murray, another eastern suburbs criminal well known to police, and seized a shotgun with a home-made pistol grip that belonged to Bertie Kidd. The shotgun had been used by Kidd in a string of home invasions and an attempted bank robbery for which, in 2004, at the age of seventy-one, he was convicted and sentenced to twelve years' jail. Kidd was a close associate of the murdered underworld figure Mick Sayers. Murray, who is two years older than Kidd, was Kidd's driver and lookout in some of the robberies. He was convicted of related crimes and jailed for three years. The shotgun had also been used in the 1991 hit on underworld figure Roy Thurgar and the 1992 hit on 56-year-old Desmond Anthony Lewis, a former boxer and standover man involved in illegal bookmaking.

In the late 1990s Skinny Mischa accidentally shot himself in the leg while playing with a gun when drunk. In an attempt to save face he at first tried to pass off the shooting as an attempted hit. A few years later, in 2003, Mischa really was the target of a gangland hit. He was shot three times as he entered an Elizabeth Bay apartment block and died instantly. At the time of his killing, Mischa was a suspect in several murders in Sydney and Wollongong.

A detective involved in the investigation of Michael Mann, Bertie Kidd, the home invasions and the murders connected with the Serbian drug ring explained how things worked: 'Double Bay is a bit like an episode of *Seinfeld*. Everything that happens seems to be linked with something else that's going on in Double Bay.'

Joe's career as an undercover cop continued, but a personal crisis was looming. Joe had earned himself a good reputation, both among the police who knew his work and among the criminals and drug dealers he mixed with in Sydney's underworld. But the strain of keeping his two lives apart was beginning to tell.

A girlfriend of several years, who we will call Nina, left him. Nina knew he was an undercover cop, but like Joe had kept it from her friends. She saw the changes in Joe as he struggled to separate his personal life from that of the musclebound drug dealer he was pretending to be. They argued. In the end, Nina could no longer cope with the lies she and Joe were forced to tell. Before walking out, she warned Joe about the dangerous path he was on. But Joe was too immersed in his fictional life to recognise the risks. 'Nina was the first to see the problems ahead and to try to warn me about them,' Joe says now. 'If I had listened to her, my whole life might have been different. But by the time she saw what was happening to me I think it was too late. I'd already lost the power to pull myself out of it.'

After the break-up with Nina, Joe had a few short-term relationships. His social life as an undercover cop revolved around strip clubs and men's clubs and, almost inevitably, his girlfriends came from that world. They liked 'bad boys' as long as they had plenty of cash to throw around.

Joe formed a relationship with a stripper and table dancer (we will call her Jade) in a well-known adult club in Sydney's south-west. Joe was working on a number of gangsters in the area and they often visited the club together. Jade believed Joe to be a hitman and drug dealer, and it excited her. After a while Jade asked him to accompany her to the United States as her bodyguard while she competed in the Miss Nude World 1997. Joe accepted the invitation, explaining that the passport he was travelling on—which was in his own name— was a false one. It marked another stage in the blurring of the real Joe with his criminal alter ego.

But Joe was not the only person feeling the stress of living a lie. His parents, both practising Muslims, were respected in the local Arabic community. Proud to have seen their son sworn in as a New South Wales police officer, they were now the only two members of his family to know about his undercover work. They struggled to cope with the cover story that Joe had left the police under a cloud and was suspected of corruption by the Wood Royal Commission. This news had spread quickly through Sydney's Arabic community at the time Joe went undercover. His parents knew the truth but couldn't say anything.

Joe's parents were also profoundly aware of the changes in his personality and behaviour. He was gaining a reputation for being a gangster and that was how he behaved. While his parents had the sympathy and support of their broader family and friends, they were forbidden to explain the reasons for their wayward son's behaviour.

They knew that Joe was risking his life for the good of the community and public shame was a cost they had to bear for his sake.

Joe's identification with the underworld was now so great that he began to enjoy acting like a thug. He revelled in the respect he had won from real gangsters—and he envied their money. Cash went through their hands like water. Although Joe was reimbursed for some of his expenses, much of his police wage went on his gangster image—the expensive clothes and jewellery and braided hair—and on living the high life expected of a successful drug dealer. The gym was now the centre of his existence.

It's like the stock exchange. Whatever it is you're after—big or small, legal or illegal—the gym is the place to go. Buying or selling, it's all the same. Either there's a bloke in the gym who can help you, or else he knows someone who can. If you're in the know you get the VIP treatment. I modelled my cover story on the targets I saw and worked on. The big guys were the ones to know. Being big made me someone to reckon with. I could walk around Sydney's meanest streets and into drug dens with no problem. I never had to worry about people intimidating me. Rather it was a matter of who I was going to intimidate.

By 1998 Joe's sense of his true identity had completely broken down: he could no longer see himself beneath the disguise.

I had become the final product of my undercover work. A little bit from this target, a little bit from that. I was the finished article. I was king. Everyone knew me or wanted to know me. I was respected in the drug world and as an undercover cop that is all you strive for: to win the respect of the dealers because you're a dealer yourself. Once you have their respect you can tell them it is day when it is night and they will believe you. But in becoming that person I'd lost sight of the other part of me, the real me, who'd become a cop because he could see what drugs and crime had done to his community. I was trying to put dealers away but at the same time I was one of them, and I enjoyed it.

Joe Pistone, the Federal Bureau of Investigation agent whose infiltration of the US mafia was depicted in the 1997 film *Donnie Brasco*, experienced a similar transformation. The longer he spent undercover, the more he identified with the mobsters and their way of life. Describing the change, Pistone said, 'All my life I've tried to be the good guy, the guy in the white fucking hat. And for what? For nothing. I'm not becoming like them [mafia wiseguys]; I am them.'

Chapter 7
Partners

In August 1997 Joe was approached by Superintendent John Dolan and another former colleague, both of whom were now attached to the Special Crime and Internal Affairs (SCIA) command. They asked Joe to join a new 'elite' undercover unit intended to track down corrupt police who had escaped the Wood Royal Commission. Justice Wood's recommendations would lead to some of the most profound reforms in the history of the New South Wales Police and SCIA was to play a central role in the shake-up. Assistant Commissioner Mal Brammer was appointed its commander, reporting directly to the Deputy Commissioner Specialist Operations. With the enthusiastic endorsement of the new commissioner, Peter Ryan, SCIA's charter was expanded under Brammer to cover the investigation of organised crime. Organised crime, Brammer argued, could not exist without police corruption, and SCIA could not tackle one without also tackling the other.

On 2 October 1997 Joe began work at SCIA's Covert Operations Unit, which was housed in a building on Sydney's lower north shore. Although surrounded by shops and houses, it felt strangely cut off from the outside world—far more cut off than anywhere else Joe had worked. Secrecy was paramount. This time Joe was warned not to mix even with fellow undercover police.

Some of his former colleagues in the Special Services Group resented his move to the new unit, seeing him as a competitor rather than a colleague. Others, like Detective Sergeant (later Deputy Commissioner) Nick Kaldas, were genuinely concerned for Joe's welfare. They knew much more than Joe about the pressures of undercover work and were aware of the special risks it posed to young operatives. Kaldas had recently completed a review of covert operations. After identifying serious flaws, he proposed significant changes to both operational and welfare procedures. In his review Kaldas noted that: 'Historically, the Undercover Unit's focus in New South Wales has primarily been drug enforcement, with a certain "ownership" of the unit in that field to the exclusion of others ... There is ample anecdotal evidence of non-drug investigators being unable to access undercover operatives' services to any great extent.'

Rather than a centralised system of undercover recruitment, 'Selection of candidates for undercover courses (and thus eventual undercover duties) has rested with each of the five regions in the New South Wales Police Service, independently.' The result, Kaldas concluded, was that selection had been 'less than satisfactory and far from consistent' and 'ad hoc undercover units' had sprung up across the police service. His solution to this 'ad hoc' undercover system was to establish a single undercover unit that better served the 'whole' of the police, and to initiate 'a fundamental shift in focus for every phase of undercover policing, from selection and training to the "nuts and bolts" of where, when and for whom the operatives are to be utilised.'

Despite Kaldas's recommendation that there should be a single undercover unit to serve the whole of the police, Brammer convinced Commissioner Ryan that SCIA should have its own discrete undercover unit. Ryan gave top priority to SCIA and its new undercover unit and Joe was glad to be part of it. The unit was to be a flagship of the 'new' police, and a primary mechanism through which the commissioner would complete the work started by the Wood Royal Commission.

One of Joe's first assignments for SCIA was at an inner-city gym where Tom Domican trained. A number of young police attached to organised crime task forces trained at the same gym and some of them either corruptly or naively were socialising with Domican and giving him information about their operations.

Domican had been mentioned numerous times at the recently closed Wood Royal Commission as a standover man with criminal interests in Kings Cross and elsewhere. The well-known Kings Cross criminal Louis Bayeh told people that he had been paying for protection and that if there was a 'war' in Kings Cross, Domican would take his side.

A survivor of the gang war that tore through Sydney's underworld during the mid-1980s, Domican had learned how to look after himself. As a result of the gang war he was charged with one murder, one attempted murder and five counts of conspiring to murder. Domican spent several years in jail defending the charges, but after the trials and appeals were over he was acquitted of the lot. He was not the sort of man to miss an opportunity to cultivate police for information and to use that information to enhance his status in the underworld.

In December 1992 Domican had organised a meeting on behalf of Louis Bayeh with then Assistant Commissioner Col Cole, head of SCIA's predecessor, the Office of Professional Responsibility, and with then President of the Police Association of New South Wales, Tony Day. The object of the meeting, it was later said, was to discuss a contract supposed to have been taken out on Bayeh's life by police. Two years later the lunch and other relationships between police and criminals were investigated by the New South Wales Independent Commission Against Corruption. A criminal informant told the commission that 'Domican was going around town boasting that he had [Assistant Commissioner] Cole in his pocket.' The commission was satisfied that nothing improper occurred at the lunch, but concluded that 'the fact of the lunch became known amongst the criminal fraternity, in such a manner as to increase Domican's apparent influence'.

During the early 2000s, the Australian Crime Commission conducted Operation Barrator, which investigated a multi-state organised crime network of which Domican was said to be an active and senior member. In its 2003 Annual Report, the commission described the network as operating 'against a criminal backdrop of pervasiveness, resilience, entrepreneurialism and corruption—all features which make it difficult for law enforcement to effectively disrupt organised criminal activities.'

During his time at the gym Joe became friendly with Domican. At first Domican peppered him with questions about his background, where he lived, what he did for a living and so on, but Joe's answers must have satisfied him, and Domican—who rarely trusted anyone—seemed to believe that Joe was a crook who could be trusted. He also appeared genuinely impressed with Joe's body size and performance in the gym. It must have been obvious to Domican that Joe was using steroids.

Their conversations revolved around criminal activities, but Domican was careful not to admit to anything—although this didn't stop him boasting about being a man who had contacts and could 'get things done'. The Domican assignment achieved little in professional terms but marked a significant personal turning point for Joe. He was starting to lose his ability to distinguish between targets and friends. He liked Domican and considered him to be 'a good bloke'. Later, Domican would do a big favour for Joe, proving that he was indeed a man who could 'get things done'.

It was shortly after this that Joe met Jessie. She arrived at SCIA at a critical time in his life, when the strain of working long periods undercover had begun to effect profound changes in Joe's personality that mirrored the changes in his appearance. During his two years at the drug squad, Joe's body weight had virtually doubled—mainly as a result of the steroids he was using. He had a wardrobe full of designer clothes he could scarcely afford and drove a midnight blue BMW 320 paid for out of his police expenses.

Emotionally, he felt empty. He had neither a girlfriend nor anyone else he could confide in. He had invested everything he had in a life that was not his, among people he could not trust, to achieve results that were unpredictable and often unsatisfactory.

Joe's isolation left him exposed in his undercover work. For the gangsters he mixed with, an attractive girlfriend was an accessory, like the jewellery and the luxury car. Joe needed a partner to watch his back, a colleague whose skill and judgement he could depend on. But more than that, he needed a friend, someone who understood the pressures of the job and with whom, at least while they were alone, he did not have to pretend to be someone he was not. In Jessie, he was to find both.

Jessie was working as a detective at Kogarah when Gary Richmond, head of the investigations unit within the Professional Integrity Branch of SCIA, invited her to join the unit. Richmond was a civilian. He had previously been a member of the Tasmanian police, and had spent a number of years at the National Crime Authority. He had relatively little experience in investigation, particularly major crime and covert operations. He and another officer comprised the selection panel and do not appear to have had any expert guidance to help them with that process.

After a few quick questions Jessie was told 'You'll do,' and offered an undercover job. Because of the nature of her work— she would be investigating corrupt cops—Jessie would not be trained with other undercover police but would be sent to do her training in Queensland, where she would not come into contact with police she might one day have to investigate.

Before she could finish her training Jessie was ordered to begin part-time work—without field support—as an undercover operative at SCIA. Her first targets were Senior

Constable Anthony Dilorenzo and Constable Rodney Podesta of Bondi local area command, both of whom were suspected drug users and dealers.

Jessie was told to visit the bars, clubs, coffee shops and other places frequented by Dilorenzo and Podesta in order to infiltrate their networks and pick up whatever intelligence she could. About 7 am on Sunday 28 June 1997, just a few weeks after Jessie had joined the operation, 33-year-old Roni Levi, a photographer, ran into the surf at Bondi Beach holding a large knife. Police were called. As Levi walked out of the surf and onto the sand he was surrounded by six police with guns drawn. Among the police were Podesta and Dilorenzo. After a thirty-minute stand-off Podesta and Dilorenzo each fired two shots, killing Levi on the spot. Friends told police Levi had been suicidal. He had sought help from Sydney's St Vincent's Hospital the previous night but left without seeing a doctor. Allegations soon emerged that Podesta and Dilorenzo may have been affected by drugs when they shot Levi; neither officer was drug-tested at the time.

A public furore followed the shooting. SCIA intensified their investigation of Podesta and Dilorenzo and Jessie was offered a full-time undercover position in SCIA's Covert Operations Unit. She was told that she was one of only two operatives selected for the unit. Officially, Jessie was now attached to Flemington as a full-time detective. The transfer to the covert unit had to be secret, so only the local area commander was told the real story. Jessie cleared her desk at Flemington and slipped away, leaving puzzled colleagues to pick up the pieces of her unfinished investigations. For her own safety she was told not to associate with other police— even those she considered friends.

When I started investigating Dilorenzo and Podesta I was able to live in my own flat, see my friends, go wherever I liked. I suppose I was naive about what undercover work really entailed. I got a buzz out of the operation but at the end of the day I could go home and put it all behind me. I was working undercover but in my mind I was probably still wearing a uniform. When I looked at myself in the mirror I saw a police officer. I hadn't crossed the line where things start to blur. I still thought the dangers of being an undercover cop were all physical. It takes a while before you realise the other dangers. You lose your friends. You stop seeing your family. When you're out on a job there's always someone watching your back but when you get home you're on your own. They tell you to forget the person you used to be but they don't tell you how.

These were the hard lessons that awaited her at SCIA. But joining SCIA was to transform Jessie's life in another way. At

SCIA, Joe joined Jessie in her surveillance of constables Podesta and Dilorenzo. They made a good team. The investigation continued for another twelve months and identified several other police involved in the use and supply of drugs including cannabis, cocaine and ecstasy, and connected through friends to a wider network of drug users and suppliers.

Meanwhile the Police Integrity Commission began an inquiry, codenamed Operation Saigon, into the police investigation of the shooting of Roni Levi and the alleged use and supply of prohibited drugs by members of the New South Wales Police Service. Two years later the commission found that information gathered by SCIA about the drug activities of constables Podesta and Dilorenzo had been withheld from the police Shooting Investigation Team at the direction of SCIA's commander, Mal Brammer, although they also found that there was no specific guideline requiring that information to be shared. 'There was some confusion in relation to the line of command in SCIA and a breakdown of communication between SCIA and the Shooting Investigation Team,' the commission found. The result was that 'the Shooting Investigation Team was not advised of crucial information in relation to Podesta and Dilorenzo'. Brammer explained that a critical factor in his decision not to pass on the information was his concern that there might be 'whales in the bay'—a common police term that usually refers to suspected leaks.

Commissioner Ryan did not appear before the commission, but in a submission made on his behalf he insisted there was 'no undue secrecy' and argued that 'Brammer and his command had to be flexible and make discrete decisions, and respond to circumstances as they arose.'

The commission rejected Brammer's explanation for not passing on the information to the Shooting Investigation Team and in doing so rejected Ryan's claim that there was no undue secrecy. The commission pointed out that within weeks of the Levi shooting SCIA had evidence that both Podesta and Dilorenzo were aware of the investigation into their drug activities. The commission was of the opinion that 'there were major deficiencies in the passing of information from one part of the police service [SCIA] to another [the police Shooting Investigation Team] and that there had been an 'excessive degree of secrecy'. The commission made clear that excessive secrecy did not indicate sinister or corrupt conduct on the part of SCIA officers. The report was a clear rebuff to both Brammer and Ryan.

Commissioner Ryan and Assistant Commissioner Brammer had the chance to act on the inquiry's findings but they didn't take it. In the years to come, Joe and Jessie would pay a high price for their bosses' inaction.

Chapter 8
Kings Cross

While they worked on Podesta and Dilorenzo, Joe and Jessie were given another job: to watch the Piccolo Bar, the Café Amsterdam and a number of other Kings Cross bars and cafés suspected of selling drugs. There were suspicions at SCIA that the cafés and bars were being permitted by police to sell drugs, possibly in return for the payment of protection money.

A walk around the Cross and a couple of cups of coffee confirmed at least the first part of the briefing: drugs, particularly cannabis, were being sold openly over the counter in several places. As Jessie and Joe noted, in some places it seemed that more cannabis than coffee was being sold and no attempt was made to hide the deals. The Dutch-style Café

Amsterdam in Roslyn Street, about 200 metres from the Kings Cross police station, was the most blatant of the drug shops. A sign declaring the café to be a 'great joint' hung in the window. 'It was almost as if the owner felt untouchable,' Jessie recalls. 'It made both of us nervous. If the police were turning a blind eye to what was going on in there, you had to ask yourself why. We had the feeling from the beginning that we weren't being given the whole story.'

The nearby Piccolo Bar had a history going back to the early 1950s. A popular hangout for the bohemian set, as well as businessmen and locals, it was recognised as a place to get a good cup of coffee, a meal—or 'something else'. The bar kept a low profile and caused little trouble for the police or local residents. In return, the police were willing to ignore the 'something else' that was being sold there.

Joe and Jessie made drug buys at various bars and cafés, saw drug use and sales, and captured some of these activities on videotape. It quickly became obvious that the sale of drugs in some of the bars and cafés, such as the Amsterdam and the Piccolo, was well known to local police—it could hardly have been otherwise. The smell of cannabis regularly wafted across the footpath as uniformed police walked past, looking the other way.

One day in June 1998 Jessie and Joe visited Café Amsterdam. As usual they recorded what they saw before leaving the café around midday. About half an hour later, as they were having lunch in a nearby café, they saw local police and drug sniffer dogs raid the Amsterdam. Several people were arrested. They reported the raid to their supervisor, who denied all knowledge of it and told them to stick to their job. But he was lying. The raid was the result of information given to local police by SCIA. During their time in Café Amsterdam that morning Joe and Jessie had unwittingly been watching other undercover police (who were not aware of being watched) buying cannabis in preparation for the afternoon raid. In another example of excessive secrecy, Joe and Jessie had been left out of the loop.

Not surprisingly, it worried them. Joe and Jessie wondered what else was being kept from them. While they had not found proof of police corruption, they had seen ample evidence that police were turning a blind eye to drug activity in the area. They also had evidence of drug distribution that, although relatively small in terms of the quantity sold in each transaction, totalled a large amount during the course of a day—enough to generate substantial profits for the sellers. Now, as if all their work counted for nothing, they had been told by their supervisors to pack up and move on.

Further raids were carried out on the Amsterdam and other places but two years later the cafés were flourishing. In June 2000 the *Daily Telegraph* ran a story headlined 'COFFEE POT—Drugs are on the menu at five city cafes'. The newspaper had found evidence of drug sales 'inside the

Piccolo Bar, Café Amsterdam and the Café Elysee. The staff of two new businesses—Café 7 and the Bliss House Café—also sell cannabis.' According to the *Telegraph*, a staff member at the Bliss House Café had boasted that 'sales in the café will gross $1 million in its first year of trading'. Prices quoted in the article revealed that in some of the cafés a gram of cannabis cost less than a cup of coffee and in the Piccolo Bar less than half the cost of a beer. The following day, 14 June, police raided three of the five cafés named in the *Daily Telegraph* article. To nobody's amazement, no drugs were found. Several of these cafés have since changed ownership.

It would be another ten years before Joe and Jessie learned the truth about the Kings Cross operation. SCIA knew that Constable Rodney Podesta had previously worked as a waiter at the Piccolo Bar and that his father, Joe (since deceased), had been the owner. Joe had sold the bar in 1994, the year before Podesta joined the police, but SCIA wanted to know whether Podesta's time in the bar had influenced his drug habits and whether he was using a network operating out of the bar for his current drug activities. None of this information had been given to Joe or Jessie, who had no inkling of the Podesta connection. (In fact Podesta's association with the Piccolo turned out to have ended when his father sold the bar.)

The Kings Cross operation took Joe and Jessie back into a world they were familiar with, but it also exposed them to something new: the world of the homeless, the street kids and drunks, and the mentally ill who haunted the lanes and alleys around the strip clubs and all-night bars.

Late at night and early in the morning Jessie and Joe saw the homeless sleeping in parks and doorways, often huddled together for warmth and protection. Most were alcoholics or chronic drug addicts; many suffered from mental health problems. Joe's BMW, his clothes, gold jewellery and seemingly endless supply of money attracted the attention of some of these down-and-outers. At first he and Jessie gave them a dollar or two 'just to get rid of them'. But over time they developed an empathy for these unfortunates. They saw their helplessness, their despair, their vulnerability. They watched the coins they handed over being spent not on food but on drugs and alcohol, and recognised that to these people drugs were not a form of recreation but an escape from lives that were otherwise unendurable.

Two homeless Aboriginal men—both alcoholics—were always keen to come over for a chat. No doubt the thought of a dollar was uppermost in their minds, but as the weeks went by it became clear both men were happy simply to have someone to talk to. Sometimes Joe and Jessie shouted them to a cheap meal, but they had to be careful. Their image on the streets of Kings Cross was that of an underworld couple, a drug dealer and his ritzy girlfriend. It wouldn't do for either of them to be seen as a soft touch for the homeless.

One afternoon Joe and Jessie were near the Piccolo Bar when they recognised one of the two homeless Aboriginals staggering down the street, obviously drunk and trying to cadge a cigarette. One man took offence at being asked. After a noisy altercation he threw a punch. The Aboriginal man fell to the ground, hitting his head. As he lay there bleeding, passers-by either stepped over or walked around him, while the assailant finished his own cigarette before walking into a bar. Other homeless people eventually came to the injured man's aid.

A few days later Joe and Jessie saw the injured man's friend. He was alone. It was early morning and he was already drunk. 'He's dead,' the man told Jessie. 'They killed my mate.' Then he stumbled off down the street. Jessie and Joe just looked at each other. For all the millions of dollars in gambling and drug money that washed around the Cross, here was a man who'd been bashed to death for the price of a cigarette. It was a side of Kings Cross most people never saw, although it was staring them in the face.

*

On Friday 29 May 1998 Joe and Jessie were out cruising the cafés, bars and nightclubs of Kings Cross and Paddington. Officially they were off duty but tonight they were mixing business and pleasure, looking for a couple of targets and picking up any intelligence they could. In the early hours of

Saturday morning they were sitting outside the Kink Café in Oxford Street, Paddington, not far from the Goodbar nightclub. The usual young crowd was milling on the footpath outside the club when gunshots rang out. Joe looked around to see a man he recognised as Bassam Hamzy, an Auburn drug dealer and standover man, waving a pistol and chasing a young man who was wounded and screaming. Others were either part of the chase or simply following the action. A little further down the street the young man tripped and fell in a shop doorway. Joe and Jessie watched in horror as Hamzy stood over him and calmly shot him in the back before firing a couple more shots into the air and running off.

Their instinct was to give chase but, as undercover cops, they knew they couldn't. 'We had spent months in the Cross working on different jobs,' Jessie recalls. 'Breaking cover now would have meant throwing all that work away. Who knew what the consequences of that might be?' In any case, their police training told them not to run blindly after the shooter when they didn't know the background to the incident. And there was another problem: they were unarmed.

'I never carried a gun,' says Joe. 'Walking around Kings Cross with a gun at four o'clock in the morning would have put me at extra risk. When criminals know you carry a gun they get the urge to carry one themselves. Besides, if I was stopped and searched by police a gun would have created problems I could do without. After a while I realised that being big gave me all the advantage I needed. A gun makes you dangerous, so an opponent has to make sure you won't use it—by shooting you if he has to.'

Local police were quickly on the scene. The murdered man was eighteen-year-old Kris Toumazis. Later that day Joe and Jessie found out that Nicholas Lambos, Toumazis's mate, had also been shot.

Joe and Jessie gave a detailed account of the shooting to a supervisor at SCIA, who told them they had been right not to break their cover. The matter was not raised again with either Joe or Jessie. They were never told whether their information had been passed on to the investigating police. Later, supervisors at SCIA denied to an internal police inquiry that they had been given any information about the murder by either Jessie or Joe.

Even without their help, police quickly identified Hamzy as the killer. Despite what their supervisor had told them, Joe and Jessie were tormented by the idea that they could have prevented the murder. By focusing on the big picture and refusing to get involved, had they been partly to blame for Toumazis's death?

After the shooting, Hamzy fled to Melbourne before leaving the country. He travelled through Lebanon, Belize and Colombia before being arrested in Miami, Florida, and extradited to Australia. Two and a half years later, in July 2001, Hamzy was convicted of murdering Toumazis and wounding Nicholas Lambos and sentenced to a total of twenty-one years' jail.

In Goulburn's top-security Super Max jail convicted triple murderer Michael Kanaan added Hamzy to the gang of killers he was recruiting to take control of the jail from the inside. On 10 November 2002, in an article headlined 'How triple murderer set up a payroll system in prison', Alex Mitchell of the *Sun Herald* quoted the then Opposition corrective services spokesman, Michael Richardson, describing Kanaan, Hamzy and 31-year-old convicted double murderer Vester Fernando as being 'among the most dangerous killers in the NSW prison system'. According to Richardson, Kanaan was 'recruiting a gang of murderous enforcers to use as his lieutenants. He was the leader of a vicious, violent gang when he was on the streets and now he is rebuilding his gang inside jail.'

Hamzy immersed himself in the study of radical Islam and became the powerbroker and self-appointed imam. Jail inmates were seen kneeling in front of him and kissing his hands. As Stephen Gibbs noted in the *Sydney Morning Herald* in November 2005: 'At Super Max their brothers in Islam include the alleged terrorist Faheem Lodhi, triple killer Michael Kanaan, his fellow gang members and killers Rabeeh Mawas and Wassim El-Assaad, killer Mohamed Rustom and pack rapist Bilal Skaf.'

About a dozen of the three dozen inmates in Super Max were Muslim, Gibbs reported. Two years later the head of corrective services, Ron Woodham, described Hamzy as one of the worst criminals he had ever come across. Photographs of the al-Qaeda leader, Osama bin Laden, were confiscated from Hamzy's cell and he was transferred to a part of the jail where he did not have contact with other inmates. He was allowed non-contact visits only and required to speak in English during visits and telephone calls.

In December 2008 Hamzy and seven others, including several members of his family, were arrested and charged over the operation of a drug manufacturing and distribution network that sold around $250,000 worth of cocaine, ice and cannabis each week in Sydney and Melbourne. Hamzy ran the operation from his maximum security jail cell at Lithgow. A mobile phone had been smuggled into the jail. Over six weeks police and jail authorities monitored Hamzy making around 19,000 telephone calls from his cell—an average of 460 calls a day—as he directed the drug operation. At the time of writing, Hamzy and his alleged co-conspirators were awaiting the outcome of court proceedings against them.

Thirteen months before his arrest in 2008 over the jail-based drug operation Hamzy and another prisoner sought to sue the head of corrective services, arguing that their segregation in jail was a deprivation of liberty. In April 2009 the Supreme Court ruled that they had a strong enough case for it to be heard. On hearing the decision Hamzy 'gleefully shouted, "I fucked the Commissioner",' according to Harriet

Alexander of the *Sydney Morning Herald*. However, a few months later the state government introduced retrospective legislation confirming 'the reasonable practices of the Department of Corrective Services' and closing the loophole that might have enabled Hamzy and his fellow prisoner to succeed in their action.

*

Several years after the Toumazis shooting, Jessie was having her hair done at a place she had been going to for years when the two hairdressers started talking to her about the murder of Kris Toumazis. By this time Jessie was out of undercover work and they knew her to be a police officer. Jessie was stunned to hear one of them say: 'Kris was my husband's cousin.' She sat in silence as the two women talked about how the murder had affected the Toumazis family. Guilty memories of her failure to prevent the murder came flooding back. Jessie never returned to that hairdresser.

Chapter 9
Craig Haeusler

Being an undercover cop is never without risk but working in your home town—as Jessie quickly found out—greatly magnifies the dangers. During an undercover operation in Darlinghurst, Jessie was startled to hear her real name being called. With her standard undercover accessories of fake tan, fake nails and dyed hair or wig, the last thing Jessie expected was to be picked as a cop. Looking casually over her shoulder, she realised that she was being followed by a police officer she recognised as a fellow trainee from the academy. As she had been trained to do, Jessie ignored him and began walking faster, hoping to lose him among the pedestrians in Oxford Street.

My heart was racing. He was a cop at the Darlinghurst station. Just talking to him would have destroyed my cover in a second. In any case I didn't want to face him and have to explain all the rumours about how I'd gone bad and had blown my career in the police. I always had this fear in the back of my mind that sooner or later I'd be recognised by someone who knew me and I'd have to make myself scarce or talk my way out of it but I never dreamed the person would be another cop. I didn't know what to do. He kept calling me and trying to catch up. The faster I walked, the faster he walked. It was like the Keystone Cops, but I was terrified.

I could hardly start running down Oxford Street so I ducked into a beauty salon and pretended to look at the products on the shelf. I was hoping he'd realise that he must have been wrong. The next thing I knew he had his face against the window, trying to see if it was me. I asked the shop assistant if they had a back exit. She could see I was shaking and asked me what was wrong. I told her the man outside was stalking me. She and another staff member whisked me out the back and through a rear exit. They were obviously worried and wanted to call the police. I said, 'No, no! Don't call the police. I'll be all right.' They shut the door behind me and I left as fast as I could.

In early 1998 Jessie's covert vehicle was broken into and the door locks were damaged. After she reported the incident to her supervisor, he notified Brammer, who told her to report the incident at a police station under her covert identity. Brammer saw it as a good opportunity to start building credibility for Jessie's covert identity by entering her false name on the police computer. But there were plenty of police in Sydney who knew her: what if one of them recognised her? Brammer ignored her misgivings. 'Report the matter to Glebe,' he said.

Reluctantly, Jessie did as she was told. But her fears proved to be well founded. Soon after leaving Glebe police station she received a phone call from the commander of the station on her covert phone—the number she had given when reporting the incident. He wanted to know why she had used a fake name. Just as Jessie had worried, another officer at the station had recognised her. Following her supervisor's instructions, she denied it. The Glebe commander accused her of lying and demanded to know whether Jessie was conducting an integrity test on his officers. Again she stuck to her guns and denied being a police officer. The irate commander reported her to Internal Affairs and Jessie was forced to change her covert identity, her vehicle, her phone number—everything.

The bosses had a good laugh about it but to me the whole experience was humiliating. I'd followed orders and where had it got me? These blokes were supposed to be the best, they had absolute control over undercover operations, and all they'd done was make a fool of me. If that was the way they handled a trivial matter, how would they behave when something serious was at stake? I was relatively new to undercover work but already I was beginning to ask myself how far I could trust them. I started to understand what it was like being an outsider in the police force, working beyond the boundaries, without a uniform to protect you.

Early in 1998 Joe and Jessie were given a new target: 37-year-old Craig Haeusler, the central figure in a multi-million dollar amphetamine production and distribution operation based in Sydney's eastern suburbs. Joe knew about the Haeusler network from his time at the Drug Enforcement Agency, almost a year earlier.

During the first half of 1997 Joe had met and done some business with 'Ray', a drug supplier with connections to a major eastern suburbs drug network which operated across much of New South Wales and Queensland. One of its principals was Haeusler. In May Ray introduced Joe to a supplier named 'Ben'. They met in the Biggles Bar of the Park Royal Hotel at Mascot. Ben was a trim, affable man about fifty years old. After a short conversation he handed Joe two plastic resealable bags, one containing five ecstasy tablets and the other a small amount of speed. The drugs were samples organised by Ray and were supposed to lead to larger buys.

Ben told Joe that he got his ecstasy from the 5T gang in Cabramatta, but he felt they were unreliable suppliers because they were more concerned with selling heroin. Ben said, 'I've got two thousand E's right now, if you want them.' As always, Joe insisted on testing the samples before committing himself to the buy. Ben told him the price: 'The speed is $1000 to $1200 an ounce, coke is $3700 to $4200 an ounce, and the E's are $24 each for a thousand, but negotiable above that.' After exchanging numbers and setting down some rules for not talking on the phone, Joe and Ben left the hotel.

About three weeks later Joe rang Ben and told him the samples were 'no good'. They agreed to meet at the Zetland Hotel in Mascot the following afternoon.

Not surprisingly, Ben wasn't happy. 'What's the problem?' he asked.

'Mate, the stuff was very bad,' said Joe. 'Actually it was a waste of a trip. That's how bad it was.'

'Yeah? I spoke to the guys and they told me they were selling it in the thousands.' He paused. 'I'll be honest with you, mate, I did get one or two complaints. But it's all I've got at the moment.'

'I don't know where you're getting your stuff from but the speed wasn't crash hot either. It had a bit of kick, but it didn't last. If that's all you've got you can count me out.'

'What about coke?'

'It would have to be better than the others. But if the quality was good I could be interested.'

'How interested?'

'A couple of ounces.'

After an unpromising beginning, Ben seemed satisfied with how the meeting had gone.

Meanwhile, on Joe's side, events were moving fast. Joe knew that a much bigger operation was under way into Craig Haeusler's drug operations, but nobody had bothered to give him the details. In fact the Haeusler investigation had made some important breakthroughs that resulted in Joe's efforts being completely overtaken. During the second half of 1997 and the early part of 1998 Haeusler and around forty others, including three serving New South Wales police officers, had been arrested and charged with several counts of supplying amphetamines. In related operations around twenty-five other members of the network were charged with supplying and manufacturing amphetamines. At the time of his 1997 arrest, Haeusler and three others were under remand for the manufacture and supply of methylamphetamine during 1994—13 kilograms of the drug had been found in their laboratory at Beaconsfield in Sydney's southern suburbs.

The swoop on Haeusler came just in time for Ben. So far, apart from delivering a few samples, his relationship with Joe was all talk. No significant amount of drugs had changed hands. The charges available against Ben were too minor to justify breaking Joe's cover. As a result, he escaped arrest. Joe was disappointed by the failure to catch Ben but the experience reminded him that he was part of a team involving many other police and that his personal objectives might not be the same as those of the team.

Out on bail, Haeusler went straight back into the amphetamine trade. There were too many customers wanting his product and too much cash to be made for Haeusler to walk away. Despite the disruptions caused by the police, his manufacturing and distribution network was still largely intact. This time Joe's target was to be Haeusler himself.

One of Haeusler's favourite restaurants was Joanna's, in the inner-Sydney suburb of Surry Hills. As well as gangsters and other underworld characters, Joanna's was a favourite of politicians and lawyers. In the early 2000s it was described on its website as 'Sydney's most exclusive lingerie restaurant. Established in 1993, Joanna's has been host to a discerning business clientele for nine years, serving up tasteful erotic shows, a gourmet a la carte luncheon and sensual lingerie waitresses.'

Haeusler was married with children but had a girlfriend who worked at the restaurant. Tania Stenberg was twenty-seven years old, tall and dark-eyed with shoulder-length brown hair. She became friendly with Joe and told him about her past, which was as colourful as Haeusler's. Two former boyfriends had been murdered in gangland disputes while a third, 32-year-old customs officer Paul Alexander Kellaway, had been arrested and sentenced to four years' jail for supplying ecstasy, lysergic acid (LSD) tabs, amphetamines and cannabis. Released after eighteen months, Kellaway established an escort agency for wealthy businessmen and set up a cocaine, ecstasy, amphetamine and cannabis distribution network in Sydney's eastern suburbs. Arrested again, Kellaway pleaded guilty in 2006 to two drug trafficking conspiracies and numerous drug supply charges. He was sentenced to a total of twelve years' jail.

Joe insinuated himself easily into the crowd at Joanna's and didn't have to wait long for an introduction to Haeusler. On the afternoon of Friday 13 February Joe was at the club having a drink with a few regulars when Haeusler joined the group. He was very relaxed and talkative.

'I used to be like you,' Haeusler told Joe, 'the flashy jewellery and the flashy clothes. But I had some problems with the [New South Wales] Crime Commission.'

'What's the Crime Commission?' asked Joe.

'It's like court. They ask you where you got your assets from and if you tell them they can't use it against you in criminal court.'

'Then they seize the assets, right?'

'The bastards took a fortune from me. But you keep something back, don't you? I mean, you never tell them everything.'

They laughed. It was obvious to Joe that Haeusler had a bad coke habit. He openly sniffed lines in front of others, some of whom joined him.

Another key figure in the Haeusler network was 48-year-old Richard James Simpson. Simpson had been an amphetamine user since the early 1980s. During a period when it was in short supply he had researched alternative methods of manufacturing the drug. By the mid-1980s Simpson was doing around six 'cooks' a year, each producing around half a pound of high-quality amphetamines. As his reputation spread, the scale of his cooks grew and he became part of a loose manufacturing network. He met Haeusler, who was already involved in the amphetamine trade, and Haeusler became a supplier of chemicals, an occasional cook, and a major seller of their product. Increasing demand led to more cooks being trained. The expanded network found ready customers in outlaw motorcycle gangs including the Black Uhlans, the Comancheros and the Bandidos, as well as other criminal groups.

At the height of the Sydney gang war of the mid-1980s, Simpson was introduced to Reginald 'Mick' O'Brien through Barry 'Sugar' Croft, an amphetamine and heroin distributor for Barry James McCann. O'Brien had been a close associate of Robert 'Aussie Bob' Trimbole since the 1970s. Like Trimbole, O'Brien had been a familiar figure at the racetrack, gambling, training horses and mixing with some of Sydney's more notorious racing identities. By the late 1970s O'Brien was using inside information and rigging races to ensure that Trimbole won. He was also heavily involved in the drug trade. After Trimbole fled Australia in 1982, he was visited six times by O'Brien in Italy, France, Switzerland and Spain. On each trip O'Brien carried with him—or got someone else to carry—a suitcase containing hundreds of thousands of dollars in cash for Trimbole. Once he was accompanied by Trimbole's son, Craig—an association O'Brien hoped would lead to better things.

With Bob Trimbole out of the country, O'Brien's income dried up and he offered his services as a man with contacts to the East Coast Milieu, a loose affiliation of eastern suburbs crime figures whose primary focus was drug importation and trafficking. But the money was not enough.

O'Brien introduced Simpson to Craig Trimbole, who claimed to have access to precursor chemicals for the production of amphetamines through a contact in a chemical company. But either Trimbole was exaggerating his influence or the contact got cold feet because nothing came of the discussions.

It didn't bother Simpson, who was already stocked up with the necessary chemicals and wasted no time preparing for a cook at O'Brien's stables at Granville. Over four days, with help from Croft and O'Brien, Simpson produced about 10 kilograms of high-grade amphetamines worth about $1 million if sold in bulk or ten times that if diluted to 10 per cent purity and sold on the street. But O'Brien was not satisfied. He had expected more and accused Simpson of ripping him off. In a rage he pulled a gun and sprayed the lab with bullets. No one was injured, but it spelt the end of their business relationship.

The break-up turned out to be lucky for Simpson. A couple of years later O'Brien rolled over to the National Crime Authority and several of his mates in the East Coast Milieu were arrested. He later withdrew his evidence and none was convicted.

Two years later, with the gang war in full swing, Sugar Croft was driving his car on City Road, Chippendale, when he stopped at the intersection of Myrtle Street. Another car drew alongside and two shots were fired, one of which struck Croft in the head, killing him instantly. Arthur Stanley 'Neddy' Smith was charged with the murder of Croft and six others, but the charge of murdering Croft was thrown out at committal.

In January 1992, at the age of forty-nine, O'Brien was assassinated—shot once in his Granville unit with a heavy calibre handgun. The night before his murder, O'Brien had made several phone calls. One was to Ann Marie Presland, who, for fifteen years, had been Bob Trimbole's lover. No one has ever been charged with O'Brien's murder but according to the coroner there was 'an abundance of suspects'.

In 1991 Simpson was arrested for operating a clandestine laboratory, but beat the charges. Three years later he was arrested for operating another clandestine laboratory. The cooks continued as he worked his way through the court system.

With Simpson's trial approaching, in December 1995 Haeusler introduced him to Bill Duff, a corrupt former New South Wales detective who had been sacked for his role in a plot to import drugs through Papua New Guinea. At the time he met Simpson, Duff was under remand for a 1994 charge of supplying heroin worth an estimated $40,000. With Haeusler vouching for him, Duff persuaded Simpson to teach him the tricks of the amphetamine trade. At the same time he introduced another former police officer, Bill El Azzi, to Simpson as someone who could advise him on ways to attack the police evidence in his drug case. In return El Azzi joined Duff in becoming an apprentice cook.

Even as his trial began in February 1996, Simpson went on cooking. At one point during the trial, he even had his bail conditions changed to enable him to spend the weekend in the country where a cook was being carried out.

Despite El Azzi's efforts, Simpson was convicted of manufacturing and supplying amphetamines and sentenced to eighteen months' jail. The cooks went on in his absence.

While in prison Simpson received regular visits from his wife Helen, El Azzi and other members of the network and was able to provide them with invaluable advice on technical problems. By the time Joe began working on Craig Haeusler, Simpson was on day release from jail. Released on parole in mid-1998, Simpson went straight back to full-time cooking. Haeusler was happy to see his old mate back on the job: not all cooks were equal and Simpson was one of the best.

Over the next few months Joe saw Haeusler several times at Joanna's and at various nightclubs in Kings Cross and Bondi. One evening Jessie arranged to meet Joe in the city for a meal. What happened next could have been disastrous for both of them.

Several months earlier SCIA had noticed Haeusler and his wife advertising for a babysitter. Seeing a golden opportunity to get inside the Haeusler household, SCIA asked Jessie to apply for the job. Calling herself Mia, Jessie was interviewed by Haeusler and his wife. While Mrs Haeusler asked questions about Jessie's experience with children, her husband spent most of the time looking at Jessie's breasts. In the end Jessie didn't get the job—Mrs Haeusler said she was looking for someone older—and SCIA missed the chance to eavesdrop on Haeusler from inside his own home.

The restaurant Joe and Jessie chose was a well-known restaurant in Sydney's east. While waiting to be seated, Joe spotted Haeusler, who immediately beckoned him over. There was no time to back out. Jessie's heart raced as Joe introduced her to Haeusler. Would he remember her face, or the false name—Mia—she had used when applying for the job of babysitter? What would she say if he did? Fortunately Haeusler was in party mode—high on drugs or alcohol or both. Next to him was his girlfriend, Tania. There was no sign of Mrs Haeusler. He didn't recognise Jessie as he invited her and Joe to join the group.

Haeusler was his usual garrulous self. From time to time he broke off the conversation and disappeared to the toilets to snort a line of cocaine. Others got up and followed, knowing that Haeusler was in a sharing mood. Each would make their own lines and sniff them. The few who went there to use the toilet paid little attention. 'It wasn't just Haeusler's party who were sniffing,' Joe recalls. 'Everyone was doing it. Sometimes there was a queue and even Haeusler would have to line up and wait his turn.'

Once or twice Joe raised the possibility of doing business but Haeusler kept putting him off, saying, 'Let me get to know you first.' Haeusler's apparent friendliness, his open use of cocaine, his ready access to and seemingly constant possession of more drugs than he could personally use, and his bounteous supply of free drugs to friends all seemed to contradict his caution when it came to discussing business. Haeusler's weekly costs had to run into several thousand, Joe thought. In order to make that kind of money he must have a very profitable operation—so profitable that he had no need to jeopardise it by introducing a new player.

In December 1998, four years after their arrest over the Beaconsfield drug seizure and at the end of a five-week trial, Haeusler and his three co-accused were convicted of manufacturing and supplying methylamphetamine. Haeusler was sentenced to seven years' jail and an additional term of one year and nine months. The judge had granted him a 30 per cent discount to reflect the undisclosed 'assistance' he gave to law enforcement authorities.

Haeusler's distribution network collapsed soon afterwards. It was broken with a series of raids and arrests that continued until mid-1999. The raids identified about fifty different sites around Sydney that had been used as drug laboratories. Each site had been used, on average, for three cooks. More than 200 kilograms of pure methylamphetamine—or about 2000 kilograms of street level 'meth' worth around $200,000,000—was estimated to have been produced and sold over a ten-year period. This did not take into account large quantities of ecstasy that had also been produced and sold. Nor did it include the 50 kilograms of pure methylamphetamine that was in the process of being manufactured at the time of the 1999 arrests. More than thirty people were charged. All but a handful went to jail.

Duff, who was believed to have carried out one cook and was preparing for another, was jailed for three years in November 1997 over the 1994 heroin supply charge. He was still on parole when, in June 1999, he was arrested over the amphetamine cook, but the charges were eventually dropped.

El Azzi was charged in 1999 with conspiring to manufacture amphetamines. It took more than forty court appearances over four years before he was convicted and sentenced to seven years' jail. The main witness against El Azzi was Simpson, who had discovered that El Azzi was having an affair with his wife.

Simpson had not been long out of jail when, in 1998, he was contacted by David Kelleher, former partner of Arthur 'Neddy' Smith in the heroin trade. Kelleher was in jail but it didn't stop him arranging a meeting between Simpson and Graham 'Abo' Henry, another of Neddy's old business partners. Abo and Simpson met at an Auburn pub where Abo asked Simpson to do a cook for him. Abo promised to provide all the chemicals—all Simpson had to do was give him a shopping list—but Simpson turned down the offer. Abo kept asking but Simpson was too busy doing cooks for Haeusler and the bikies to take on any more work.

In June 1999 Simpson pleaded guilty to manufacturing amphetamines and was sentenced to four years' jail. The judge strongly recommended that the prisoner spend his time in custody on strict protection due to what he called 'special circumstances'.

*

Back on the streets in 2006, Haeusler quickly set about rebuilding his life of crime. Despite the efforts of the Crime Commission, he still had significant assets and was living comfortably. He was also alleged to have 150 kilograms of pure pseudoephedrine that had been hidden in secure storage since before his jailing. It was worth between $3 and $4 million on the illegal drug market as a precursor in the manufacture of amphetamine. Cooked, it was enough to produce around 90 kilograms of amphetamine/methylamphetamine worth around $90 million on the street. It was cash that Haeusler would be only too happy to accept, as compensation for his time in jail and insurance against future arrests, but there were catches. As he put the word around he had to be careful to distinguish between those who were genuinely interested in buying and those who were more interested in ripping him off—using extreme violence if necessary. There was also the risk that the Crime Commission might still be looking at him.

Although their efforts did not result in arrests, the intelligence gathered by Joe and Jessie was useful in monitoring Haeusler and his associates and contributed to other operations. Due to the paranoid secrecy at SCIA, neither

Joe nor Jessie was debriefed on the Haeusler operation. It was only while researching this book that they learned the extent of the network and realised the dangers involved in trying to penetrate it. One piece of information in particular would have given them pause for thought.

Without an arrest to bring them to an end, undercover operations can either run on indefinitely or else drift to an ambiguous close. While working on Haeusler, Joe retained a lingering interest in Tom Domican. What Joe didn't know was that Domican was in regular contact with both Haeusler and other senior members of his network. Domican was also a close associate of El Azzi. The danger for Joe was that he had been using different names and different cover stories for the Domican and Haeusler operations. There was a real risk, while he was with one, of accidentally bumping into the other. If that happened, not only would both operations have been blown, but Joe's life would have been in danger.

Sydney's underworld is a small place and Joe's time in it had left him badly exposed. In the circumstances it seemed just as well for him and Jessie that they were about to be given a new assignment that would take them thousands of kilometres away, to the coast of north Queensland. The job, however, would turn their lives upside down.

Chapter 10
Mackay

In late 1997 the Queensland Criminal Justice Commission (forerunner of the Crime and Misconduct Commission) began Operation Craven, an investigation into the distribution and use of drugs and protection of criminals by Queensland police in the Mackay area of north Queensland. A year later the commission determined the investigation should move to a new phase that would involve the use of undercover police. Meanwhile, in New South Wales, Joe and Jessie were told the Kings Cross job was over and other Sydney-based jobs were to be put on hold. In November 1998, after talks between the New South Wales Police and the commission, both were assigned to Craven.

Joe pointed out to his handlers that he had now been working undercover for three years—a year longer than the recommended maximum—but his concerns were brushed aside. Craven was an important job, they told him. He would be given all the help he needed.

Joe and Jessie talked the matter over. This wasn't the rest Joe felt he needed, but it was a fresh start in a place neither of them knew. By now both were disillusioned with their jobs at SCIA. The extreme secrecy within SCIA precluded any kind of team spirit. They felt they were being kept in the dark—or even actively misinformed—by their handlers. Jobs were assigned and then, without explanation, called off. Serious criminals had been allowed to escape arrest and Joe's and Jessie's safety put at risk for the sake of investigations that seemingly had gone nowhere. Things could not be worse in Queensland, they told themselves, and if Operation Craven was as important as people said it was it would allow them to put their disappointments at SCIA behind them.

In November 1998 Joe went to Brisbane to meet his bosses at the Criminal Justice Commission. He was told that Operation Craven was an investigation into police involvement in drug trafficking in north Queensland. Detectives in Mackay had allegedly given protection to a bikie gang operating in the area. Joe was also told that Jessie would not be joining him. She had completed her undercover training during 1998 in Queensland and there was a risk of her being recognised.

This was bad news for Joe, who had come to see Jessie as the one person he could rely on. Nevertheless, Jessie urged him to fly to Mackay to check out the area and get a feel for the place. During their time together she had come to trust his professional judgement. If Joe thought the job was a 'goer', the chances were he was right.

During the few days he was there, Joe sensed that something was going on. In fact Mackay had a long history of police corruption. In the early 1950s Constable Jack Herbert, who would later become notorious as the 'bagman' who collected bribes for corrupt police including the commissioner, was assigned to Mackay. Herbert described what he found on his arrival: 'There was a hotel across the street from the police station. As well as eating there, we drank at the hotel during and after hours ... On our way to eat in the dining room on race days, we had to push through crowds betting with an [illegal] off-course bookmaker. Even with my limited experience, I knew this wouldn't be happening unless the local police had agreed to look the other way.'

A decade after the Fitzgerald Inquiry blew the lid on police corruption in Queensland, Operation Craven was about to demonstrate that it was back again, only this time the focus wasn't illegal gambling and prostitution, but drugs.

Over the next few months Joe travelled between Sydney, Brisbane and Mackay, assessing the prospects for the Queensland job while undertaking with Jessie a couple of Sydney jobs, one of which focused on allegations of corruption by Assistant Commissioner Clive Small and his alleged association with a Sydney crime boss (see Chapter 12).

By February 1999 Joe was spending most of each week in Queensland, returning to work on Small on Friday evenings and during the weekend. His handlers, meanwhile, had had a change of heart about Jessie. It was going to be a long job and Joe would be expected to have a girlfriend. Taking Jessie would save him from the risks inherent in picking up a 'handbag' in Mackay. In April, Jessie joined Joe in Mackay.

Joe's first task was to find long-term accommodation. He wanted somewhere far enough from the city to give them space when they needed it, but close enough to keep them at the centre of the action. The place he chose was the Shores Holiday Apartments at Blacks Beach, a fifteen-minute drive from Mackay. This would be his and Jessie's home for the next ten months. Hidden cameras and electronic recording devices were set up in the apartment, and door and window locks double-checked. Jessie recalls:

We were supposed to be a couple, so that was how we had to set up the apartment. We had a double bed in one room, and a big wardrobe with all our clothes. Obviously it had to look as if we were sleeping together, even though we weren't. There was a spare bed in the other room and either Joe or I slept there. If we were ever caught sleeping in different rooms, the cover story was that we'd just had a big argument. It wasn't easy, living together and pretending to be lovers when we were just colleagues. With some undercover jobs you can go back to your own home at the end of the day. But in Mackay we were with each other nearly all the time. Even when we weren't together, we had to stay in character. I had to be Joe's handbag whether I was with him or not. In practice the situation can go one of two ways—either both of you get on each other's nerves so much that the professional relationship breaks down, or else you end up becoming what you're pretending to be. For a while neither of us was sure which way it would go.

Once settled into their apartment, they quickly set about finding a gym. The gym they chose was used by several Mackay police and a number of local drug dealers, who were also well known at the town's more popular nightspots. As gym regulars, they soon worked their way into the city's night-life. Over the next few months Joe and Jessie became familiar faces in Mackay's bars and nightclubs, befriending any locals they thought might be able to help them. One of these was Constable Gerard 'Gerry' McArthur.

From the outset it had been clear to Joe that steroids were easy to get in Mackay. Other gym users spoke openly about them. Joe bided his time, waiting a few weeks before making his first move. One day he asked a gym regular—we will call him John—about the availability of goey (amphetamines). John answered, 'There's one guy I know who uses a spot and he's going for six to eight hours ... Peter is the guy you should talk to. I'm seeing him today. I know he sells a spot [local jargon for a taste and an expensive way to buy amphetamine] for $50 and a gram for $150.'

Peter was Peter James Whitten, a local dealer. Over the next few days, Joe raised the possibility of an introduction but was told that Peter was cautious and would not risk a meeting. When Joe asked about the local police, John laughed. 'Put it this way,' said John, 'Peter sells to half of the coppers around here.'

'Really? He used to sell or still does?'

'Still does, to the young coppers. Mate, they can't get enough. They used to be even worse.'

'What happened?'

'There was a big bust at Airlie Beach. They caught a whole bunch and swept through to Mackay. That cleaned them up a little.'

Over the next few months Joe ran into Peter several times in the gym and around town. Peter was a big man, 184 centimetres tall and roughly 130 kilograms, with a shaved head. At twenty-eight, he took his fitness very seriously. 'He was very aggressive and arrogant in the gym,' Joe recalls. 'He intimidated other patrons; not smiling or talking to anyone smaller than him, treating them as if they were beneath him.'

Peter worked as a bouncer at a popular nightspot called the Saloon Bar. Joe and Peter acknowledged one another but it was three months before they exchanged more than a handful of words. One day, after a workout in the gym, their regular casual greeting developed into a conversation about the availability of amphetamines. 'There's a fair bit around,' Peter said. 'It's pretty good.' So far he wasn't saying anything that Joe didn't know already. Joe waited for him to go on. 'If you're interested,' Peter said, 'I can get some for you.' They agreed on a sample.

Four days later, around 11 am on Friday 18 June 1999, Joe met Peter in the car park of McDonald's in Shakespeare Street. They went for a drive in Peter's car—Peter was concerned about police surveillance—and discussed drug deals and the local police. They talked generally about opportunities in the drug trade in Mackay and Peter told Joe that he only used one supplier, who got his drugs from the local chapter of the Rebels outlaw motorcycle gang.

'Yeah,' said Peter. 'They [the local police] know about me and what I do. I sell to a lot of them. Not wiz [methylamphetamine], but steroids and fantasy.' (Fantasy is a white powder taken by bodybuilders to lose body fat. When mixed with alcohol it works like speed. It is also known as grievous bodily harm, GBH, liquid ecstasy, and a variety of other names.)

'That's the way,' Joe agreed. 'Have them onside.'

'Yeah,' said Peter. 'They leave me alone. The Brisbane cops fly up here two or three times a year and they [the local police] let me know when they are coming.'

'It sounds like you've got it all sorted.'

'I do all right ... I should warn you, mate—the local boys have been talking about you.'

'You mean the cops?'

'Yeah. You want to be careful.'

'Thanks for the tip.'

'Do you want a [drug] testing kit?'

'Where from?' asked Joe.

'I get legit ones from the cops,' Peter said. 'They come in boxes of three and they take a couple out.'

A drug-testing kit was a useful accessory, allowing a dealer to carry out on-the-spot tests to confirm that he was buying the real thing and not being ripped off. For Joe a kit would be doubly useful, saving him from having to taste the drug and supporting his claim not to be a user and to be in the drug business only for the money.

'How much?' Joe asked.

'About twenty bucks.'

'Sure. I'll have a couple.'

Joe looked at the samples of cannabis and speed Peter had given him. 'I'll place an order once I've checked them out, but I can tell you now I'll need twenty to thirty pounds of grass and at least half an ounce of speed to make it worth my while.'

'Shouldn't be a problem.'

The conversation switched to steroids—Peter confessed to using about $600 worth of steroids a week now that he was back in the gym 'in a serious way'.

Later Peter dropped Joe back at McDonald's. As he drove home to Blacks Beach, Joe felt pretty pleased with himself. He had been in Mackay for five months and his patience had paid off. He had found out that there was a flourishing drug trade in the town and that the police were part of it. And by biding his time, he'd dealt himself into the game.

Around this time something happened in Sydney that was profoundly unsettling for Joe and Jessie: their New South Wales supervisor changed. It seemed like a routine switch: their supervisor had been promoted and Detective Sergeant Graeme Pickering was appointed in his place. They had nothing personal against Pickering, but neither of them knew him. Building a relationship of trust and confidence with a stranger when they were 1800 kilometres apart was not going to be easy. The decision, however, was out of their hands and all they could do was go along with it.

A safe house had been established in Blacks Beach, close to Joe and Jessie's apartment. It was used by their New South

Wales supervisor when he was in Queensland. From now on that person would be Pickering. His cover story was that he was a consultant named 'Geoff Patterson'.

The landlady's husband was often away cutting cane and it wasn't long before Pickering started taking advantage of his absence. The affair between Pickering and his landlady was quickly noticed by Joe and Jessie, who feared that the clandestine relationship might compromise the operation and, worse still, jeopardise their lives. For Joe and Jessie, the safe house was no longer safe.

They challenged Pickering about the affair: 'We're concerned about your relationship with [name deleted]. You're going to blow us and the job.'

Pickering was dismissive, denying there was an affair. His high-handed attitude only added to their fears. At the very moment the operation had started producing results, they realised they could not depend on their supervisor. They felt alone and vulnerable. Perhaps it was inevitable that Joe and Jessie would turn to each other for the emotional support they both desperately needed. Until now they had been careful not to act on the physical attraction they felt for each other: they had enough problems already, they thought, without compromising their professional partnership by becoming emotionally involved. Yet their dependence on each other already went far beyond that of colleagues. Becoming the lovers they were pretending to be was not a convenience but an acknowledgement of a deep trust they had come to share during their time in Queensland.

*

On the afternoon of 30 August, while working out at the gym, Peter approached Joe. It was six weeks since he had given Joe the samples. At last he was ready to deal.

'Have you got four five?'

'What do you mean?' Joe asked.

'Have you got it or do you have to go to the bank?'

'Yes, I have it.'

'I'll see the guy and give you a call.'

In the world of drug dealers, success is often judged by the size of your wallet and the tips you leave. Carrying large amounts of cash brings a risk of being robbed or ripped off by other crooks, but the risk of not having money can be even greater. The would-be drug dealer without cash is quite likely to be taken for a cop. For the past two years Joe had made it a rule to carry several thousand dollars in cash at all times. Since the police bean counters didn't look kindly on non-itemised expenses, the money was always his own. Throughout the Mackay job, Joe kept around $5000 hidden in their apartment. Typically, on the afternoon Peter proposed the deal, Joe's supervisor was in Brisbane and unable to provide the cash. A delay would have looked suspicious, so Joe used his own money.

Two hours later, Peter called. 'Cool to come and see you?'

'Yeah,' said Joe.

There was no back-up so Joe and Jessie devised their own emergency plan. Joe hid his gun under a cushion on the lounge where he would be sitting. The furniture was arranged so that Peter would be given a low armchair that restricted his ability to make sudden movements. Jessie's gun would be hidden in the kitchen or in the bedroom. As soon as Joe and Peter started discussing the deal, Jessie would make an excuse and leave the room. If there was any trouble, both Joe and Jessie would have access to weapons. Peter would be covered from two different angles.

Half an hour later Peter arrived at the Blacks Beach apartment. He was nervous and suspicious. 'Have you got the cops waiting for me when I leave?' he joked.

'Yeah,' said Joe, 'and they're coming in for a cup of coffee.'

'I usually don't deal with people unless I've known them for five years or more,' Peter replied, before producing a bag of cannabis and scales from a holdall. The cannabis weighed 458 grams and Joe paid Peter $4400.

The deal done, they talked about future possibilities. Joe asked about 'Gerry [Constable Gerard McArthur] the policeman'.

'He's a crook,' said Peter. 'I've sold him about seven to eight ounces of fantasy which he takes to the Gold Coast and sells to other police. The last time I sold to him was about two months ago ... I've got four people selling for me. If I have any trouble with them I get the local boys [the police] to pay them a visit and get them out of town.'

After Peter had left, Joe wondered whether he had been bragging. But his allegations of police drug dealing were consistent with what John had told him in the gym. Maybe Peter had been exaggerating, but the gist of what he'd told Joe was probably true.

Two weeks later, on 13 September, Peter had something to show Joe. He asked Joe to call around to his home and showed him a sample of speed. 'It's better than that other sample I gave you,' he said. 'Do you want it or not?'

'Okay,' said Joe. 'It looks pretty good.'

The next morning Peter approached Joe in the gym. '[I] got that thing for you. I picked it up this morning.'

After training, they left the gym in Peter's car. Peter did his usual anti-surveillance checks, driving around in circles until he was satisfied he was not being followed, before parking in an open area near the mouth of the Pioneer River, which flows through Mackay. He gave Joe a small amount of speed and guaranteed the ounce that Joe wanted would be of the same high quality. Joe gave him $200 for the sample and they agreed on $5600 for the ounce.

By now Joe and Jessie were seeing Peter regularly, but despite the deal Joe sensed that Peter didn't entirely trust him. A week after the $200 buy, still waiting for the promised ounce, Joe joined Peter and a friend in a bar in Mackay. Peter was in good spirits. 'I made about thirty [drug] deals today,' he boasted. He introduced Joe to his companion, a local drug user and a small-time dealer. After a while they were joined by Jessie and a couple of others. They each had a few drinks. Peter started popping ecstasy pills and offered one to Joe. At first Joe declined, but Peter was insistent. He gave Joe a pill and watched to see if he took it. It was a tricky situation familiar to any undercover cop working in the drug trade. Refusing to take a free pill when it has been offered is tantamount to pulling out your police badge.

Previously Joe had used the line that he was only in the trade to make money and didn't believe in consuming his own profits. But he could see that Peter was not going to accept that story. Some operatives end up using drugs to avoid blowing their cover, but not Joe. This time he was lucky. He was able to convince the half-drunk and drug-affected Peter that he had swallowed the pill. He even gave Peter $50 for it. Peter was still throwing down shots of sambuca and vodka, with chasers of bourbon and Coke, when Joe and Jessie called it a night around 2 am.

The next day Peter rang Joe. After complaining that he was 'still recovering' he told Joe that he'd got the 'gear' and wanted to come over within the hour. It was about 6 pm on

Sunday 26 September when Peter arrived at the Blacks Beach apartment and gave Joe a bag of amphetamine. It weighed 17 grams and was in a red 'gluggy' form indicating that it was fresh and had not been cut to reduce its purity. This was not what Joe expected, but Peter assured Joe that it was quality stuff. Following a short discussion about the price, they agreed on $2900 and Joe handed over the cash.

For several months Joe and Peter had been discussing the advantages and risks—mostly in terms of financial costs—of having police 'onside'. Peter explained his philosophy: 'Like anything, it's a jungle and you have to scratch their back for them to scratch yours. If you look like shit they hassle you, but if you're respectable they leave you alone.'

This Sunday Joe decided it was time for him to test Peter. He asked whether Peter could get his mates in the police to check a Queensland car registration number for him. Joe explained that it was a car that he had 'an interest in'. The next day Peter came back with the information: he had proven to Joe that he did have corrupt police contacts. This was another breakthrough. But what Joe and Jessie were not aware of was that six weeks earlier Peter had asked his police mates to run police and road traffic checks on Joe. The falsified records organised by the Queensland handlers had gone a long way to convincing Peter and his partners that Joe and Jessie were okay.

A month later, on 22 October, Gerry called at the Blacks Beach apartment. They had met a few times before but this was the first time they had discussed their relationship with Peter, corruption and their involvement in the drug trade. Joe knew Peter supplied drugs to Gerry, who was both a supplier and user.

'You know what I'm doing, don't you—what I'm up to?' Joe said.

'Yeah.'

'You know I'm buying drugs from Peter [Whitten].'

'I heard something about that.'

Joe was fairly sure that if Gerry knew about the deals, it was because Peter had told him. They discussed how unreliable Peter could be. Then Joe turned the conversation to the Gold Coast. 'Do you know any police on the Gold Coast who can give me protection for a [drug] transaction?'

'There's a bloke down there doing the same as me,' said Gerry. 'He'd do it if I asked him.'

'What's he like?'

'Put it this way: if it was me I'd do the deal in Brisbane. The protection would be 100 per cent.'

Joe agreed to switch the transaction, provided protection could be arranged. Realising that Gerry was the police contact who had done the rego check for Peter, Joe gave him a Nokia mobile phone 'as a gift'.

Later that night Joe and Gerry hooked up again for a drink. In the Saloon Bar they saw about fifteen police. Gerry spoke with several of them. The presence of so many police made Joe uncomfortable. He knew a few of them personally and recognised others.

'I don't think some of these guys like me,' Joe said.

'Bullshit,' said Gerry. 'I'm the most senior here and they'll like who I tell them to like.' They both laughed. But Joe was puzzled by Gerry's attitude. Here was a fairly junior police officer who Joe knew to be corrupt, a drug user and dealer, flaunting his relationship with someone he was corruptly involved with and for whom he was in the process of arranging protection for drug deals. It was very risky behaviour—the behaviour of someone who believed he was invulnerable.

Two days later Joe received a tip-off about forty-year-old Russell Peter Lemberg, a major drug supplier with connections to local bikie gangs. Joe had started taking an interest in Lemberg more than six months earlier. He had seen him in the gym occasionally and with the aim of trying to 'bump into him' had been visiting the bars, clubs and eateries where Lemberg liked to hang out. Lemberg was a voracious gambler who put hundreds and at times thousands of dollars through the pokies. Joe had deliberately played alongside him and they had discussed their luck, or lack of it, on the machines. As a result of his efforts Joe had become a familiar face to Lemberg. But he was still waiting for the break that would get him into Lemberg's social circle. He knew that being seen with the 'right' people would, sooner or later, create the opportunity to establish a relationship with him.

The tip-off Joe received was the name of a hotel where Lemberg was known to drink. That night Joe went to the hotel. As usual, Lemberg was playing the pokies. Joe waited his moment before sitting down next to him. Lemberg talked about having won $1500 on the pokies the day before, but said he was now putting it all back. The conversation seemed to be friendlier than usual. For Joe it was time to make a move.

'You look like a man in the know,' he told Lemberg. 'Do you know where I can get some stuff?'

'What stuff were you after?'

'Some wiz [methylamphetamine].'

'I could help you out,' said Lemberg. 'How much do you want?'

'An ounce. For starters.'

'I could manage that.'

'How much?'

'Five and a half [$5500].'

'What about five?'

Lemberg agreed.

Joe asked when he could see a sample and to his surprise Lemberg replied, 'What are you doing now?'

They left the club and Lemberg—suspicious of being followed by police—drove through back streets and in circles to his home. The twenty-minute journey would have taken half as long without the anti-surveillance tactics. They were accompanied by Lemberg's girlfriend and his ten-year-old son who had also been in the club.

When they arrived at the house another woman was waiting outside, a 45-year-old drug user and friend. Inside, Lemberg took Joe to the bedroom where he retrieved a plastic resealable bag containing half an ounce of wiz in white powder form from a study table drawer. He gave Joe an 'electronic magnifying telescope' for a closer look. 'It's pretty good,' Lemberg said. 'I don't cut anything.'

Lemberg put a small sample of the wiz in another plastic bag which he gave to Joe.

'Got many customers?' asked Joe.

'Too many,' replied Lemberg. 'I don't like dealing with small-timers.'

He walked out of the bedroom and returned seconds later with another bag of wiz, this time in the form of brown powder. 'I've got this too,' he said.

Joe took the bag and looked at the brown wiz. 'I've bought it before but I prefer the white crystal.'

Lemberg shrugged and took the bag back. 'Suit yourself.'

Joe asked how long it would take to get the ounce he had ordered.

'Not long,' said Lemberg. 'Tomorrow or the next day.'

With the first buy agreed, Joe turned the conversation to the next. Lemberg assured him that a constant supply was available and that his source was in Brisbane. 'I haven't got a cook,' he said. 'Too much heat on me up here.'

While Joe was happy with the outcome of the meeting, he knew he'd taken a chance. He'd gone to Lemberg's home without surveillance and without having been briefed on the layout. He had no idea whether or not there were guns in the house, or whether Lemberg was luring him into a trap. Lemberg had strong links to the Rebels bikie gang. He was a dangerous customer to be tackling without back-up.

The next day Joe rang Lemberg and asked, 'Can I get that one off you?'

Lemberg turned up at the Blacks Beach apartment about 3.15 pm on his Triumph motorcycle. He knocked on the door and checked that everything was okay before returning to his bike and pulling from the underside of its frame a packet strapped on with black electrical tape. He gave the packet to Joe. It was the ounce of high-quality wiz that Joe had ordered. He paid Lemberg the agreed $5000.

Before Lemberg left the apartment, Joe canvassed the possibility of him supplying 'two ounces on a regular basis'. Lemberg was circumspect. 'What's the hurry, mate? Let's just wait a few days.'

It would be a month before their next deal. In the meantime Gerry contacted Joe and told him he had spoken with his Brisbane police 'friend', Detective Senior Constable Gregory 'Catto' Catton of the sex offenders squad, who was happy to provide the 'protection' Joe needed. Over the next few days Joe and Gerry made arrangements to visit Brisbane. Gerry was going to take with him some fantasy, supplied by Peter. He asked Joe for $1000 up front as a show of good faith for Catto and his 'mate'.

'Things were going nicely,' Jessie recalls.

We were getting close to the big dealers. Maybe we were getting a bit carried away by our success, forgetting how dangerous these people really were. One night we were driving along a deserted gravel road into Mackay when a van came out of nowhere and hit us from behind. It was a heavy collision and my head was flung forwards. Joe hit the steering wheel hard. We were both petrified. Had someone rumbled us? We were buying drugs from Lemberg and Whitten and the police were involved—if the word had got out that we were cops, we were as good as dead. Even if no one suspected we were cops, there was always the chance of another dealer trying to rip us off. We were blow-ins and one of the locals might have wanted to warn us off. We only had one gun in the car. Joe grabbed it and told me to wait. I moved across to the driver's seat. If there was any trouble he told me to get away as fast as I could. I remember wishing there was another gun in the car. It was pitch black outside and I couldn't see a thing. It seemed like an eternity before

Joe opened the door. 'It's OK,' he said. 'He's just a young bloke. He wasn't looking where he was going.' I could only guess what the other driver must have thought, seeing Joe walking up to him in the dark. He was probably more scared than we were. Afterwards we tried to laugh it off but at the time it felt like a warning. If someone wanted to teach us a lesson, it wouldn't be in the city but out here in the bush, where no one would find us. A week after the crash I was still vomiting from the shock.

On 29 October Joe saw Gerry at the gym. 'I have something for you in my bag: that police drug-testing kit you wanted. I'm sorry I could only get one.'

Besides doing business, Joe and Jessie made every effort to socialise with Gerry and his wife. She knew nothing about her husband's drug activities and Gerry used to joke with Joe about the difficulty of keeping her in the dark. 'I think she's a bit suss. She gave me the third degree the other day: a hundred and one questions. A few more and I was going to ask her to read me my rights. The other day she kept asking where all the money was coming from and I told her I was well off and had money in investments.' They were sitting in a bar. Both men laughed and Gerry glanced at Jessie, who was sitting at another table. 'What about Jessie—does she know?'

'Oh yeah, she's good and switched on.'

'Good,' replied Gerry. 'I'm glad to hear that.' He lowered his voice. 'You know that thing you wanted me to do down south? It looks like I'll be able to do it this Friday. I've juggled my shifts around so I have Friday, Saturday and Sunday off.'

'Sounds good,' said Joe. 'Just let me know when you're sure.'

Later in the evening Gerry said: 'I'm glad you're not doing [drug] business in town.'

'No, mate,' Joe replied. 'It's too small.'

'I was relieved, I can tell you. Pete [Whitten] has got a good set-up: pretty successful and low-key. Another bloke trying to muscle in might have fucked things up. You know what I mean?'

'He needs to be careful,' Joe said. 'Too many people know him and what he is doing. You know he has four runners?'

'Yeah,' Gerry responded. 'It's too many.'

'Then he has the people he deals to and one day someone will get the shits and talk. You know how it is.'

A week or so later, during another evening at the Saloon Bar, Gerry suddenly asked: 'Why did you approach me?'

The question took Joe by surprise. 'I don't know,' he said. 'You looked like someone who knew the score so I thought I'd see if we could do business together. What did I have to lose? The worst that could have happened was you telling me to fuck off.'

'I could have handed you in,' said Gerry, with an edge of menace.

'I'm clean,' said Joe. 'I keep nothing with me, so you would have nothing. You would be hassling me, not hounding me. Anyway, I would have said, "Sorry, mate. I was asking for a friend." In any case, why the hypotheticals? You didn't hand me in.'

Gerry seemed happy with the explanation. 'What drugs do you want in Brizzie? … Do you want some fan [fantasy], goey [amphetamines], or E's [ecstasy tablets], so we can have a bit of fun?'

Joe ordered E's.

They were in the Saloon Bar again a few days later. 'How much fantasy are you taking down [to Brisbane]?' Joe asked.

'Don't know,' Gerry replied. 'I tried to get some steroids from Peter [Whitten] … He didn't have any. I'm going to see the guys in Brisbane, then swap some fantasy for gear [speed] … You being from Sydney, I thought you'd be doing coke. That's what you should do here. There'll be a market for it.'

'Yeah, but it would be too expensive.'

'There's a market for it in Brisbane,' said Gerry.

As they made final arrangements for the Brisbane trip, Gerry changed his mind and decided not to take any fantasy with him. He didn't give Joe any reasons. He reminded Joe about the $1000 that would have to be paid up front and

Joe asked why it couldn't wait until after the deal was done. Gerry explained that as the middleman he was vouching for Joe to the Brisbane connection as well as for the Brisbane connection to Joe. The payment was a show of good faith. The Brisbane connection was well established in the town, while Joe was a stranger. Joe finally agreed to the payment, only to be told by Gerry to hold off until they were in Brisbane because Catton and his mate 'might want more'.

Meanwhile Peter complained to Joe that there was not much gear [speed] around and no fantasy at all. Now Joe realised why Gerry was not taking any fantasy to Brisbane: Peter had not been able to supply it. Peter asked Joe for steroids as he was back in training but, borrowing Peter's line, Joe told him his source was dry.

If Peter was lying low and out of gear, Lemberg had no such worries. He and Joe bumped into one another in the street. Lemberg claimed to have some new stuff and invited Joe to have a look. They arranged to meet in a couple of days. Joe wanted to buy an ounce.

On Thursday 18 November Lemberg called at the Blacks Beach apartment. As before, he came on his Triumph motorcycle and the drug was taped to the underside of the bike's frame. He handed Joe the bag of speed and Joe gave him $5000 cash. Joe then ordered another two ounces, to be delivered in a fortnight. He talked Lemberg into dropping the price to $4800 an ounce. Joe arranged to call Lemberg a couple of days ahead. They discussed ecstasy but 'only if the price is right' and Lemberg agreed to 'look into it'. Fantasy was mentioned but Lemberg wasn't interested. As Lemberg left, Joe realised that Peter had been right about the fantasy drought.

Joe bought tickets for himself and Gerry to fly to Brisbane. Gerry was going down a day earlier than Joe in order to make sure the protection deal went off smoothly. Joe also organised a hire car for Gerry while he was in Brisbane, but the Brisbane connection was suspicious and didn't want the car.

Chapter 11
Brisbane

On 23 November 1999 Joe and Jessie flew to Brisbane and booked into the Summit Apartments. Gerry contacted Joe and assured him that everything was fixed. The arrangements, however, had changed. Gerry had decided to help himself to a piece of the protection money. Including Gerry, there were now three people providing protection— ensuring the deal went off without a hitch and that local police did not intervene—and they wanted $500 each.

Around mid-morning the next day, Gerry arrived at the Summit Apartments. With him were Detective Senior Constable Gregory 'Catto' Catton and Joshua 'Josh' Christian Sexton, a Brisbane criminal and standover man and a Thai kick-boxing expert. After going over the plan—Catto, Josh and Gerry would be seated nearby to keep watch on the transaction—all three drove to the Garden City Shopping Centre at Mount Gravatt.

Joe went to Tuscani's café, ordered a coffee and waited. A few minutes later he was approached by 'Antonio'. Over lunch Antonio handed Joe an envelope and left. It was a staged transaction masquerading as payment for a previous drug deal. Antonio was an undercover cop and the envelope contained $20,000 cash, the serial numbers of which had been recorded. Back at Joe's apartment, the cash was counted and Gerry, Catto and Josh were each given $500. Catto was given an extra $150 for three ecstasy tablets which he promised to get for Joe later in the day.

That evening Gerry, Catto and Josh returned to Joe and Jessie's apartment. Catto gave Joe his ecstasy tablets. As they sat around the dining table, Josh produced a bag of powdered amphetamine. Catto mixed it with a blue ecstasy tablet he had crushed on the table. He used his police identification card to mix the drugs. A ten-dollar note was rolled up and Catto and Josh used it to sniff the drug.

After a while the five of them left the apartment and went for a drink. Josh made several calls to organise ecstasy tablets, finally ordering five at $50 each, paid for by Catto. While Josh went off to collect the ecstasy, Gerry, Catto and Joe caught a cab to the Heaven Nightclub. They were soon joined by Josh. The club-hopping continued until 5 am.

But Gerry wanted more. He asked Joe for $200 for a prostitute. Gerry telephoned several brothels but none would supply him with a prostitute. Perhaps $200 was not enough at that time in the morning; perhaps they could tell that he was off his face with drugs and alcohol. Gerry returned to Mackay, still hung over, the same day. Joe and Jessie drove up a day later.

Back in Mackay, Gerry and Joe discussed the Brisbane trip. Gerry said they had been lucky. He also told Joe that Catto had something important to tell him. When they spoke over the phone, Catto warned Joe to be careful because 'there are undercover jobs under way on the Sunshine Coast'. He asked Joe for the names of his contacts on the Coast (100 kilometres north of Brisbane) so he could make sure they were 'sweet'. He also promised to get details of the police operations in the area. But that was not all. Catto also warned Joe about an undercover drug operation in Cairns in far north Queensland, 600 kilometres north of Mackay. He said arrests were expected within days.

The following afternoon Joe bumped into Peter Whitten, who also knew about the police operations. He told Joe the town was dry and that he was 'taking precautions'.

Lemberg, however, was not so cautious. When Joe asked for two ounces of goey, Lemberg didn't hesitate. 'No problem,' he told Joe. 'You will be impressed [with the quality].'

While waiting for Lemberg to deliver the drugs, Joe rang Catto and gave him the names of 'a couple of people' on the Sunshine Coast he was doing business with. They were fictional names with fictional profiles recorded on law enforcement and other systems (such as licence records) in order to give legitimacy to Joe's cover story. These fictional profiles had another important function: by having the names on a computer the authorities were able to track the names of anyone who checked on them.

The next day Catto rang Joe and told him 'Cairns is cool'—someone had tipped him off that the undercover job there was over. A few days later Catto phoned again to say that 'everything was sweet' with the Sunshine Coast names, but he had to do one more check 'to be 100 per cent sure'. The following week he told Joe that [name withheld] was 'OK and clean', but the other person, 34-year-old James Dean, 'was bad news; very hot'. Dean, Catto said, had been charged 'by the CIB earlier this year [1999]' and was 'well known ... [you] shouldn't be seen with him'. The name alone could have raised doubts in the mind of someone more suspicious, but Catto didn't notice anything odd.

About 4.45 pm on Friday 3 December, Lemberg called at the Blacks Beach apartment. Joe gave him $9800 for two ounces of methylamphetamine. With the money in his pocket, Lemberg was eager to talk. He told Joe that he had been dealing in drugs for a long time and had done a couple of years' jail; that until recently he had been selling around three pounds of methylamphetamine a week but was now selling around half that. He never dealt with the police, he said, because he would 'feel like a dog'.

A week later, Joe found Lemberg playing the pokies in the local leagues club. He was $800 down. 'No complaints with the stuff I gave you the other day?' he asked.

'Only one,' said Joe. 'There wasn't enough of it.'

'I'll be getting more in the next few days,' said Lemberg. 'Same quality; same price. Are you interested?'

Joe agreed to another buy.

On 11 December Joe received an anxious call from Gerry. 'Mate,' he said, 'you have to be careful. On Wednesday we're knocking on doors, doing raids. You [and Jessie] had better keep your heads down for a few days.'

A few days later Gerry arranged to meet Joe for a drink. They ended up in the Saloon Bar, where Gerry told Joe that he had more news about the police raids: three places were going to be raided, 'but you're sweet'.

'Thanks, mate,' Joe replied. 'I'll be back in Sydney by then anyway.'

Gerry also had other news. He had scored a job in Brisbane. His last day in Mackay would be 20 January.

'Maybe you should move down there yourself,' he told Joe. 'It would be a shame if we had to stop doing business.'

'I don't know anyone in Brisbane. I'd be going down there cold.'

'That can be fixed,' said Gerry. 'I know a few blokes down there who could help you out.' He mentioned Detective Senior Constable Peter Reid: 'Reidy is a big player and knows everyone. If you come to Brizzie, Reid could hook you up and look after you.'

'I dunno, mate. Things are pretty good here. And Jessie likes the climate.'

'Think about it anyway.'

The conversation turned to Peter Whitten. 'I saw him at the gym today,' said Gerry. 'He is a happy chappie. He's got his regular supplier back and he is back in business.'

'I couldn't wait,' said Joe. 'I had people hassling me. I've found someone else. It's better stuff too.'

'Don't mind me asking who?'

'Russell Lemberg,' said Joe.

'Mate, Lemberg is bad news. Everyone knows him. If I were you I wouldn't be seen hanging around with him. He doesn't have any protection. Every time the bastard gets raided and stuff is found, someone else stands up and takes the rap.'

'Thanks for the warning,' said Joe.

'While we're on the subject,' said Gerry, 'if you ever need someone to do some selling, tell me. I know a reliable person.'

Joe said he'd bear it in mind.

There was something Joe needed, but it wasn't someone selling drugs for him. He and Jessie were desperate for a rest. Apart from a couple of short breaks in the Whitsundays and Noosa, they had been working almost nonstop since leaving Sydney several months earlier. The Mackay operation was going well and they had made good headway in Brisbane, but the stress of always having to watch their backs was getting to both of them. In an undercover operation like this there was no real downtime: the stakes were too high. They had been promised a decent break in Sydney and were counting down the days.

In mid-December 1999 Joe and Jessie returned to Sydney for four weeks. As well as catching up with their police supervisors, they spent time with Joe's family—hers was in Queensland—and a few friends. All Joe's family knew was that he had been in Queensland: they didn't know what he'd been doing there and Joe couldn't tell them. The need to lie to family and friends added to the mental pressure that was building inside Joe and Jessie. For Jessie the return to Sydney was especially difficult:

I was used to my twin sister being there. She was my best friend and my only family in Sydney. We'd always been close and even when I couldn't tell her the whole truth about my job, I could rely on her support. But I had bumped into her a couple of times while working undercover in Sydney, which was potentially dangerous for both of us. On top of that, people often confused us with each other. They would see me hanging around the drug scene and think it was my twin. Sometimes her friends would ask why her police officer sister was doing drugs. Of course they all assumed I was corrupt. My sister found herself having to lie to protect me and to protect herself. In the end she couldn't take it anymore and went overseas to escape. She only planned to stay away for a few months but she was gone for three years. I really missed her and I felt guilty for screwing up her life. It was bad enough having to lie myself but I hated her having to do it on my account. The thing about living a false life is that you never know how it will end and who will get caught up in the lies you have to tell. Joe and I used to talk about it all the time. You become an undercover cop thinking you can be in control, that if you're good enough at your job you can make the lies work for you. But what happens is the lies take over, they start to control you—and not just you but your friends, your family. It's like letting loose a virus: once it's out of the dish you can't call it back. You let enough people believe you are a criminal, a gangster, a drug dealer, and after a while it becomes impossible to deny it. You can even end up believing it yourself.

＊

The Sydney trip was not the break Joe and Jessie had hoped it would be. They were not allowed to forget work. Joe kept in touch with Gerry in Mackay and with Catto in Brisbane. On 11 January 2000, he received a call from Catto, who claimed to have a 'business proposition' which might interest Joe. It concerned a friend of his in Brisbane. 'Maybe it'll be a little expensive for you,' he said.

'I'd like to hear it,' Joe replied. 'I'll be up there tomorrow.'

Returning to Mackay, Joe caught up with Gerry and told him about the approach from Catto. 'This friend of his,' said Gerry, 'it'll be Reidy.' There was a certain awe in the way he spoke about Detective Peter Reid's 'power' and 'contacts'.

Gerry was in a talkative mood. After asking Joe about his holiday, he told him about a 'good mate' [name known] who was a police officer in Sydney and also about a solicitor [name known] who lived in Bondi and worked for one of Sydney's top legal firms. Whenever he visited Sydney, Gerry said, the three of them used to catch up and get 'shitfaced' on prohibited drugs.

On 18 January Joe travelled to Brisbane to catch up with Catto, but Catto was out of town. Four days later they met at the Sedgebrook Apartments in Brisbane's CBD, where Joe was staying. Catto was wary of talking inside and asked Joe to walk out onto the balcony.

What I wanted to tell you is that there is a guy I have known for a long time and he has a cook who makes wiz [methylamphetamine] and it's the best. My guy would know because he shoots it up his arm. He's a copper. He used to be undercover and they threw him out because there were allegations he was bashing drug dealers [and] taking the gear and selling it. He's a user and knows the go. I bought a hundred E's off him for $17 each and gave them to a mate to sell them for me. My guy comes back and says he has good wiz and asks me if I know anyone who's interested.

Joe stalled for a few moments, not wanting to seem too eager. 'How much?'

'$1800 for half [an ounce] and double for one.'

'You're sure he's a mate?'

'I always deal with him. His name is Reidy, Peter Reid.'

'All right,' said Joe. 'I'll take an ounce. When can we meet?'

'Leave that to me. But I'll tell you now, Reidy is very switched on. He's careful who he does business with.'

That night Joe, Catto and his girlfriend—a police officer in the drug squad—went out for a meal where they were joined by Josh Sexton and a local police officer. Later, at the Trans nightclub inside the Transcontinental Hotel, Catto introduced Joe to 'Ian', a small-time dealer who was 'looking after a few police'. Joe saw Catto give Ian some cash, probably a couple of hundred dollars. Later Catto gave Joe an ecstasy tablet. Joe offered to pay for it but Catto waved the money away: 'Don't be silly.' At the first opportunity, Joe discreetly slipped the pill into his pocket, pretending to have swallowed it and commenting on its taste.

During the evening Joe saw Ian doing a couple of deals. The police paid no attention. By then a number had already made their own purchases, from Ian or from other dealers in the room.

Reid arrived and had a conversation with Catto, then left without talking to Joe. 'That's Reidy,' Catto explained. 'He gave me two samples of E's that just came in from the [United] States.' An hour later Reid returned to the club and Joe was introduced to him. After some small talk, but no business, Reid walked over to the bar and spoke with Josh and then with Catto before leaving. Catto approached Joe and said, 'He asked me if you wanted a sample and I told him the ounce was the sample.'

During the evening several others, including some police, joined the party. Among them was 'Crazy Ray', a heavy Brisbane drug dealer in his early forties. Crazy Ray was a gym junkie and a steroid user. He made no attempt to conceal his activities. He told Joe that he used to sell in half-pound and pound lots but had scaled back and now did 'a couple of ounces here and there'. He offered Joe wiz for $800 an ounce—half the price others were demanding. Joe was suspicious: was it the real stuff or was it rubbish, or was Crazy Ray just setting him up for a rip-off?

A couple of days later Joe got a call from Gerry. 'Greg [Catton] said that Crazy offered you some stuff.'

'Yeah,' said Joe. 'Eight hundred an ounce. I asked how good it was for that price and he reckons it's pretty good.'

'I don't know with those guys,' said Gerry. 'Ray's done time. I'd stay out of it if I were you.'

Joe was content to follow Gerry's advice. Crazy Ray was a distraction. Joe's priority was Reid. He felt that Reid didn't trust—or just didn't like—him. If either was true it would make Joe's job a lot harder. 'I don't think your mate [Reid] likes me,' he told Catto.

'He's just cautious,' Catto replied. 'But fuck him. He thinks I'm not capable of knowing people who are big-timers. Don't worry about it.'

But Joe's instincts were right. A few days later Gerry and Catto came round to Joe's apartment. They told him that Reid didn't trust him. Catto had vouched for Joe but Reid was still not convinced. 'He wanted to know if I'd seen you taking any illegal drugs.'

'What did you tell him?'

'What do you think? I told him I had. But I dunno if he believed me. Reidy's a suspicious bastard.'

All this spelled serious trouble for Joe. From what Catto had just told him it was obvious that Reid was going to be a much tougher target than the others. Reid knew what undercover police could and could not do in Queensland.

Catto then told Joe about the conversation he'd had with Reid. 'He wants you to supply him with a gram of amphetamine or cocaine. He tells me if you're a dealer it won't be a problem, but if you're a copper you'll come up with a hundred and one reasons why you can't supply it. And there's another thing—he wants $5000 to $6000 upfront for twelve months' protection. He won't give any guarantees, but for that Reidy says he'll keep his ear to the ground.'

'Generous bastard, isn't he?'

'Mate, I told you Reidy was suspicious. But you're not a copper so what's the problem?'

'No problem,' said Joe. 'Only I don't like dealing with people who don't trust me.'

Joe needed to create a delay that would give him time to get instructions. He returned to Mackay to catch up with Jessie and keep that end of the operation running. While he was there something unexpected happened: Joe was approached to carry out a hit. During the night of 28 January 2000 he and Jessie were in the Saloon Bar, the same nightclub where they had mingled all year with police and drug dealers. Gerry and a few of his police colleagues were also in the bar. After a couple of drinks Joe and Jessie went off to sit by themselves. Sometime after midnight Joe was approached by a woman calling herself Sue. She had been in the bar for a while drinking with a group of regulars, but she was not drunk. Jessie was nearby, buying a drink at the bar. Sue was in her late thirties, slender and expensively dressed. After a short conversation she asked: 'What nationality are you?'

'Lebanese,' Joe replied. 'What are you?'

'Hungarian,' said Sue. 'I've been watching you all night. I want to know if you can do something for me.'

'Depends what it is.'

'I've seen you around town and I've made some inquiries about you. You're the only one who I think can do it. I need a gun and I want you to kill my boyfriend.'

For a few moments Joe thought she was joking, but the look on her face told him she was serious. 'Why?' he asked.

'He's a bad person.'

Joe decided to play along. 'All right,' he said.

'Can you do it?'

'Of course I can.'

'So you're interested?'

'I might be. But it's gonna cost you.'

'I'm ready for that. I'm sitting on a gold mine, if you know what I mean.'

It crossed Joe's mind that someone was pulling his leg—perhaps one of the men at the bar, most of whom he'd done business with. But there was a cold logic to the woman's proposal. Joe looked like and had been behaving like a gangster; he was on familiar terms with many of the drinkers in the Saloon Bar and other clubs around Mackay; he was friendly with well-connected local criminals and corrupt police. It would not be the first time an invitation to commit a serious crime had begun in this way. And none of the men at the bar looked as if they were about to burst into laughter.

Joe needed time to think: this had come out of the blue and was certainly not part of the Craven game plan. 'Give me a contact number,' he said. 'I'll ring you in the next couple of days and we can discuss it.'

Sue gave Joe a piece of paper with 'Sue' and two fixed line telephone numbers on it. She also gave Joe a mobile number.

'I'll give you a call,' he said, 'but I want you to know it's not going to be cheap.'

Jessie had been watching from nearby. She wasn't sure whether the woman was trying to pick Joe up or set him up. As she returned with her drink Sue said, 'I don't want your man. I'm just organising business.' She left the bar and caught a cab.

The next morning Joe reported the incident to his supervisors, both in Queensland and New South Wales. The message came back: 'Don't do anything. Have no further contact with the woman.'

Joe and Jessie were concerned: what if she asked someone else to carry out the hit? But the message was repeated: forget it; get on with Craven. Perhaps his supervisors knew something they were not telling Joe. Was the woman a test set up by Craven targets? Was she known to Joe's handlers? Was she even working for them? Joe and Jessie were never told and within days Joe was back in Brisbane.

*

A constant challenge for undercover cops is to provide credible cover stories that account for gaps in their movements. In order to make time to visit his handlers, Joe relied on the fact that successful traffickers were expected to have a finger in several pies at once. On 2 February Joe received a telephone call from Catto, who wanted to know where he had been. 'I thought someone had killed you,' Catto said.

Joe had his story ready. 'My life would have been a lot easier if they had.'

'What's the matter?'

'You've heard what happened in Sydney yesterday?'

'What?'

'Our federal mates have been busy with 500 kilos.' (The previous day the Australian Customs Service and Australian Federal Police had seized 500 kilograms of cocaine unloaded from a yacht at Patonga, on the Hawkesbury River, north of Sydney. The raid was receiving widespread media coverage.)

'Was that yours?' Catto asked.

'Not exactly,' said Joe. 'But I had some money involved so I'm on my way to Sydney to sort a few things out.'

'Fuck,' said Catto, obviously impressed. 'The cops aren't onto you, are they?'

'No, but I need to talk to a few people to see who fucked up.'

'Mate, if you need a hand let me know.'

'Thanks, mate. I think I can handle it.'

The truth was that Joe had been arguing with his handlers over Reid's challenge to supply him with a gram of amphetamine or coke. To Joe, his credibility as a dealer was at stake. But Detective Reid had been right: the Criminal Justice Commission would not allow Joe to supply drugs to Reid, no matter how small the amount. As a result, Reid refused to deal directly with Joe, but agreed to deal with him through Catto, whose faith in Joe was unshaken.

On 15 February Joe was in the Sedgebrook Apartments in Brisbane when Catto visited and told him there was a fair bit of ecstasy around: 'California whites, blues and green Mitsubishi' for around $25–$27 each for a hundred.

Joe told Catto that he did not want to deal with Reid 'because he's too paranoid'. Catto agreed and said he would handle Reid by telling him he was making a buy 'for the boys'.

The next day Catto called round again. He and Joe walked out onto the balcony to talk. 'Peter [Reid] has the California whites [ecstasy tablets] ready to go now for $26 for two or three hundred. He reckons he can do whatever [number] you want.'

They discussed the price and Joe placed an order for 500 tablets at $25 each. Joe also agreed to pay the $6000 in advance for twelve months' protection, provided the drug deal went through without a hitch.

On the morning of 17 February Joe received a phone call from Catto: the deal was on. At 11 am Joe, Catto and Gerry met at Garden City. After a short conversation Joe and Catto returned to Joe's car and drove off, followed by Gerry in his car. Both Gerry and Catto checked continually to make sure they were not being surveilled by police. As they drove, Joe handed Catto a plastic bag with the agreed $12,500 cash in it. Catto was looking to earn a few extra dollars for himself and told Joe that he would give Reid $11,500 and 'try and bluff him' that Joe had paid only $23 a tablet. They drove to Catto's home in Tendy Street, Logan City, on Brisbane's southern border. As they sat in the driveway, Gerry pulled up behind them in his car. Catto said nothing but did not get out of the car. He was still checking to see whether they had been followed. He told Joe he would catch up with Reid later in the day and they would hand over the drugs that night.

That afternoon Catto rang Joe. He told Joe to go out onto the balcony and not to talk in the unit.

'Mate,' he said. 'I was followed on my way to work.'

'Are you sure?'

'Of course I'm sure. It might just be a coincidence, but I'm not taking any chances.'

Catto said he wasn't coming to Joe's apartment. Instead he would arrange for Josh Sexton to deliver the ecstasy. Joe was also to give Josh the $6000 protection money for Reid.

'I dunno,' said Joe.

'Josh is okay,' Catto assured him. 'He knows everything.'

'I'd rather give it to you.'

'It's too risky.'

'I can let you in through the basement and no one will see you.'

They agreed to meet in half an hour, but Joe wasn't sure who he would be meeting: Catto or Josh.

Around 9 pm that evening Catto and Josh came to the apartment block in an unmarked police car. As arranged, Joe let them in through the basement. The three men went to the apartment. Catto handed Joe a package wrapped in paper towels. Joe put the package on the table and opened it. Inside was a resealable plastic bag containing 500 ecstasy tablets. They were not California whites but Mitsubishi greens, which were just as good. It was the tenth drug buy Joe had made in Queensland. Joe gave Catto the extra $6000 for twelve months' protection. As he had done on every other occasion, Catto insisted on taking Joe out onto the balcony.

'I think they might be onto me,' he told Joe. 'It's just a hunch. But we need to be careful.'

Catto and Josh were arrested as they left Joe's apartment, Reid a short time later. Homes and police stations were searched. The five hundred ecstasy tablets, steroids and several thousand dollars in cash were seized.

Detective Senior Constable Peter Reid of the drug squad was charged with supplying methylamphetamine, possession of cash derived from drug sales, and possession of cash suspected of being tainted property.

Detective Senior Constable Gregory Catton of the sex offenders squad was charged with three counts of corruptly receiving money, four counts of supplying methylamphetamine, and possession of cash suspected of being tainted property.

Plainclothes Constable Gerard 'Gerry' Patrick McArthur, who had just started at the Wynnum Criminal Investigation Branch, was charged with two counts of corruption, one of receiving a mobile telephone and another of receiving cash, and one count of stealing a drug-testing kit from the Queensland Police.

Josh Sexton was charged with several counts of supplying a prohibited drug.

Five weeks later Peter James Whitten was arrested in Mackay and charged with four counts of supplying methylamphetamine and one count of supplying cannabis, one count of carrying on the business of unlawfully trafficking in various drugs, one count of possession of cannabis, one count of unlawful possession of three weapons, and one count of possessing a restricted article.

Russell Peter Lemberg was arrested and charged with four counts of supplying methylamphetamine and one count of carrying on the business of unlawfully trafficking in methylamphetamine.

The operational phase of Craven finished with these arrests, leaving Joe and Jessie with mixed feelings of satisfaction and frustration. For all their success at breaking the ring of police corruption, both felt there was unfinished business. While working on Craven, Joe and Jessie had reported other allegations of police corruption and misconduct in both Queensland and New South Wales, including links with outlaw motorcycle gangs, corruption on the Gold Coast and the wider use of illegal drugs. None of these had been investigated—or, if they had been, Joe and Jessie had not been told of the results.

Isolation from family and friends, and the building of friendships based on lies and deceit, had taken their toll. Both were showing severe signs of stress that was affecting their personal relationship and risked overflowing into their professional partnership. Joe's protracted use of steroids— which he still considered a vital element of his cover—was causing its own problems. Joe was showing signs of 'roid rage' and on one occasion had punched a hole in the wall of their Blacks Beach apartment. He stormed out of the apartment threatening to kill himself with his service pistol in the nearby cane fields. Jessie rang their supervisor, but all she could really do was wait for him to calm down.

About half an hour later Joe returned to the apartment. He was remorseful but still upset. Jessie tried to comfort him. She could see that something was terribly wrong. 'Joe was falling over the edge and I didn't know how I could pull him back. It frightened me that he had a gun. I wasn't worried for my own safety but for his. He needed help but couldn't bring himself to ask for it.' It would be another two months before he saw a psychiatrist.

Joe had been undercover for four and a half years and Jessie had been undercover for three. They were no longer just colleagues. Operation Craven had been a resounding professional success: at what personal cost, Joe and Jessie were about to discover.

Chapter 12
Out of control

When Joe and Jessie started work at SCIA they knew they would be working on police—constables and sergeants, perhaps even an inspector. What they didn't expect was that they would be told to spy on the highest levels of the Police Executive. Among their surveillance targets were Detective Inspector Deborah Wallace of SCIA; Assistant Commissioner Clive Small, Commander of Crime Agencies (and co-author of this book), and the police commissioner himself, Peter Ryan. In each case Joe and Jessie were given little to go on—the 'evidence' against all three sounded to them more like hearsay, even office gossip. There would be no case number; nothing was put in writing; surveillance reports were to be delivered verbally. Each case raised grave questions about the purpose and control of undercover operations in New South Wales. On a professional level, Joe and Jessie had good reason to be worried. Since the jobs did not officially exist, who would be held accountable if they went wrong?

In May 1998—before they started work on Operation Craven—Jessie had been given the job of gathering intelligence on a husband and wife who appeared to have significant unexplained wealth. The wife worked at a western suburbs fitness centre as a trainer and her wheeler-dealer husband owned a strip club in the area. Among the regulars at the fitness centre was Detective Inspector Deborah Wallace, a senior SCIA investigator suspected of having unspecified 'improper' links with the couple.

Jessie started noticing Wallace at the gym's aerobic classes. At the end of the class, Wallace and others would often go for a walk with the trainer. It was during these walks that Jessie befriended the trainer, who told her that her husband was looking for hostesses for his club. As part of her cover story Jessie had said she was looking for part-time work, so she went to the club and applied for a job.

The club was dark and seedy. On seeing the waitresses in their skimpy skirts and even skimpier tops, Jessie started to have second thoughts. In any case, she doubted that her supervisors would approve of her doing the job. She said she would think about it and left the club.

The Wallace operation lasted seven months and Jessie reported to her supervisors after each visit to the gym, but she neither saw nor heard anything to incriminate Wallace. 'It was ridiculous,' Jessie recalls. 'She was just there to do aerobics.' The police never took any action against the fitness centre proprietors.

Joe's and Jessie's next operation targeted an even more senior officer, Assistant Commissioner Clive Small, the head of Crime Agencies. The information against Small came from the notorious criminal Arthur 'Neddy' Smith, a murderer, heroin trafficker, rapist and armed robber as well as a briber of police, who had told the New South Wales Crime Commission that Small was associating with the longtime crime figure and drug importer Michael Hurley. At the 1994–97 Wood Royal Commission into the New South Wales Police Service Hurley had been identified by both criminals and police as being a 'head honcho' of organised crime.

Jessie and Joe were told that the surveillance and filming of Small had been ordered directly by Assistant Commissioner Mal Brammer and approved by Commissioner Peter Ryan. Brammer himself was recorded as the case officer for the investigation. Jessie questioned the job from the outset—she had heard there was a 'bit of friction' between Brammer and Small—but her concerns were dismissed by her supervisor. 'You've been directed to do it by Brammer,' the supervisor told her, 'so you don't have any choice.'

Reluctantly, Joe and Jessie accepted the job. Small, they were told, met Hurley at the Woolwich Pier Hotel at Hunters Hill on Friday or Saturday nights. On the first available Friday night they made their way to the Woolwich Pier Hotel on Sydney's lower north shore. It was very different from the places they were used to. 'It was a nice little sandstone pub,' Jessie remembers, 'with a quaint little outdoor area, poker room, main bar and pool table room. The patrons all seemed to be locals. They all knew one another.' It certainly didn't look like the kind of hotel where underworld figures and corrupt police would meet and do business. Furthermore, she knew that Small was a local. He would have been recognised at once.

As they talked about the job, Joe remembered reading somewhere that Neddy Smith and his sometime partner (and sometime foe) 'Abo' Henry had been in the area, and possibly at the hotel, years before while planning the armed robbery of the Cockatoo Island payroll at nearby Woolwich wharf. Smith claimed it was Abo and two others who carried out the robbery, which netted more than $300,000 cash.

From the moment they sat down Jessie felt they 'stuck out like sore thumbs'. Nevertheless, they persevered. They were there to watch and gather intelligence, not infiltrate, and the food was good.

After several visits to the hotel, and no appearance by either Small or Hurley, Joe and Jessie again questioned their supervisor, but were told to continue. They were becoming increasingly suspicious. 'We thought it was an absurd allegation,' Jessie remembers.

Their surveillance at the hotel continued most Friday and Saturday nights from late January until mid-March 1999. During that time there was not a single sighting of Small or Hurley, either together or separately. Then suddenly, without any explanation, the operation was dropped. What Joe and Jessie were not told by their handlers was that for eighteen months before the allegations against Small were made, SCIA had had Hurley and his network under electronic and human surveillance. Yet the combined operations had not found any evidence of a connection between Hurley and Small.

Eight years earlier Smith had gone to the New South Wales Independent Commission Against Corruption (ICAC) and rolled on police who, he said, were involved in corrupt activities. Already serving a life sentence for murder, Smith claimed to feel betrayed by police who, he said, had given him the 'green light' to commit crime. Rolling on them to ICAC was Smith's revenge. But the deal ICAC made with Smith was highly restrictive. His indemnity from prosecution was limited to 'the commission of any offence, other than homicide, which any member of the New South Wales Police Service, past or present, aided, abetted, counselled or procured' and about whom Smith agreed to give evidence, either before a court or before ICAC. As a result his stories were tailored to include police as major participants in his crimes.

Smith's evidence to ICAC broadly followed the same line as his 1993 autobiography, *Neddy: The life and crimes of Arthur Stanley Smith*. But in places Smith deviated significantly from the stories he told in his book. (The book often contradicted itself between its draft and published versions.) Yet in none of his accounts of his life of crime and police corruption did he mention the connection between Hurley and Small which he revealed years later to the New South Wales Crime Commission. By then Smith had been in prison for a decade. As usual, he was trying to trade information for an early release—and, as usual, the information he offered was demonstrably false. Smith remains in jail.

Neddy's erstwhile partner, Graham 'Abo' Henry, later claimed that Neddy's allegations against police were nearly always a mixture of exaggeration and fabrication. In his 2005 book *Abo: A treacherous life*, Henry claimed that it was only the impracticality of murdering Smith and the fear that Smith would roll on him that caused him 'reluctantly' to corroborate Smith's testimony to ICAC.

Routine investigation would have revealed a more personal motive behind Neddy Smith's allegations against Small. In the late 1970s Smith was facing serious charges related to heroin trafficking. Neddy's stepbrother, 26-year-old Edwin, had been interviewed five times by arresting police but refused to make any admissions and lied to protect Neddy.

At this time Small was working at the Woodward Royal Commission into Drug Trafficking and was one of the commission investigators who persuaded Edwin to 'roll' and expose Neddy's heroin network. Edwin implicated Neddy Smith and others, told of previous heroin importations and described the network of traffickers that surrounded the Neddy Smith/William Sinclair/Warren Fellows/Paul Hayward group. In his public evidence before Justice Woodward, Edwin repeated his claims and was tested by lawyers representing a number of the drug traffickers he named. He stuck to his story and much of his evidence was corroborated. Edwin pleaded guilty to his own role in the importation and distribution of heroin and was sentenced to ten years' jail.

It was three years before Neddy's case went to court—he was released on bail after two years—and by then Edwin was a reluctant witness. He had been in jail since his arrest and feared for his life, both inside and outside jail. Edwin changed his evidence. The prosecution case then suffered another blow. The heroin discovered in Edwin's possession three years earlier, and which formed a significant part of the evidence against Neddy, was found to have been tampered with. Most of the heroin had been stolen and replaced with glucose or something similar. With the Crown case in disarray, the trial judge directed the acquittal of Smith.

Despite his acquittal, Neddy was bitter about the two years he had spent in jail—just as he is bitter about the three life sentences he is serving now. He has never forgiven Edwin for rolling on him. Nor has he forgiven Small for talking him into it. As he showed with his stories to ICAC, Smith's allegations about police corruption were often motivated by equal parts of self-interest and revenge.

The surveillance jobs on Debbie Wallace and Clive Small were a sign that things at SCIA were getting out of control. But neither prepared Joe and Jessie for the assignment they were given in mid-December 1999. During a visit to Sydney towards the end of 1999, Joe had mentioned to his supervisor that he had heard the commissioner and his wife sometimes went for a drink after work in the bar of the Marriott Hotel a few doors along from police headquarters in College Street. It was just a casual remark in the context of a general conversation and Joe thought nothing more about it. But when Joe and Jessie returned from Queensland for a Christmas break in Sydney, Joe was summoned by his supervisor. 'Brammer has a little job for you,' he said.

Joe asked what it was and the supervisor explained that he had mentioned Joe's comments about Peter Ryan and his wife to Brammer. 'He wants you to pop in to the piano bar at the Marriott and keep an eye on Ryan.'

'What does he want me to look for?' Joe asked.

'Anything. Who he meets. Who he speaks to. Brammer wants you to try and listen to the conversation to see if he is talking shop. Also, keep an eye on his wife. She's a talker under drink.'

Joe didn't like the sound of it. 'So is this official?' he asked. 'Do I make up an operation number and folder [the usual practice after being assigned a job]?'

'No, mate. Just relay it to me and I'll tell Brammer.'

'When do you want me to start?'

'Right away. Go there whenever you get a chance. Drop in at different times.'

Joe wanted to know what the commissioner was supposed to have done. He was told that Ryan had 'loose lips' and that his wife 'drinks too much'. Brammer was concerned that the Ryans might constitute a 'security leak'.

Joe discussed the job with Jessie, who warned him to be careful. It wasn't just the flimsy pretext that worried Joe. There was also the question of what might happen to him if Ryan found out. With no paperwork and no operation number, who was going to stand up for Joe against the commissioner?

Joe knew the Marriott Hotel and knew it wasn't his sort of place. He had built his undercover career on blending in with steroid-using drug dealers and gangsters. Now he was being asked to look inconspicuous among a crowd of police and public servants. Joe knew that his size and braided hair would attract attention in the Marriott. He would try to turn this to his advantage by making himself so obvious that nobody would dream he was part of an undercover surveillance operation. The other patrons would certainly be interested in him, but not suspicious. If approached, Joe would use the cover story that he had come up from Melbourne and was trying to make his way as a professional wrestler.

In the weeks before Christmas Joe visited the Marriott half a dozen times. He received some stares and comments but was never approached. He reported in person to his supervisor—no written record was kept. Whenever he was present, there was nothing abour Mrs Ryan's behaviour to support any of the supervisor's fears and there was nothing untoward in Peter Ryan's behaviour. The information was nearly always the same: 'I saw Commissioner Ryan and his wife. They were having drinks with some police and public servants from police headquarters. There were others there whom I don't know.' After each report the supervisor came back to Joe with the same message: 'Brammer is happy with what you're doing. Keep up the good work.'

Despite his reservations, Joe did as he was told until the operation fizzled out in mid-January 2000. The Ryan job was never mentioned again, but that didn't surprise Joe. He had never been told the full story about any operation he had worked on. Spying on the commissioner was simply the logical endpoint of a sequence of questionable operations that began with Wallace and Small.

*

Around 2000 Joe and Jessie began to hear stories about undercover police who had launched or were about to launch civil action against the police department. Some of the stories had a familiar ring to them: they involved drug and steroid use and lack of operational and personal support. Isolated from their colleagues in an organisation that prioritised secrecy above everything, Joe and Jessie discovered that they were not the only ones to have fallen victim to SCIA's cult of unaccountability, its often lax operational procedures and its maverick disregard for duty of care towards its undercover operatives.

Chapter 13
Back in Sydney

After Operation Craven ended in mid-February 2000, Joe and Jessie returned permanently to Sydney. While it might have seemed that Jessie, in her role as Joe's 'handbag', had played a minor part in the operation, nothing was further from the truth. Jessie had been integral to Joe's credibility. Her presence made it easier for Joe to mingle socially. She relaxed and distracted targets. Behind the scenes Jessie also contributed to tactics and kept watch on Joe in case back-up was needed. All this had made them staunchly loyal to one another.

Craven had been a long and difficult assignment, with little or no distinction between work and leisure. The Blacks Beach apartment had not been a safe house but the home of a gangster and his partner who might be holding drugs or cash. The apartment was thus a potential target for both corrupt police and criminals.

The operation had not always gone to plan but that was something all undercover cops had to get used to. The ability to improvise, to think and act on the run, was a crucial skill—perhaps the most crucial skill—in undercover work. But the problems with Operation Craven went deeper than that. One of the most serious concerned supervision and back-up from Sydney.

The affair between Pickering and the landlady of the safe house had represented a potentially disastrous breach of security but there had been other lapses. On one occasion surveillance support was cancelled mid-operation, leaving Joe in Lemberg's car and afterwards in Lemberg's home, with his girlfriend and a female drug user, making a drug buy. At other times recorded conversations were not monitored at the listening post in real time, but much later. The operational experience of some supervisors, particularly in Sydney, was questionable.

At times money had been scarce, a situation that dangerously contradicted Joe's cover story of being a successful drug dealer. This was a perennial problem for undercover operations. Successful drug dealers were expected to have ready access to both cash and drugs; they usually spent it as quickly as they made it. But having money on tap wasn't easily reconciled with orthodox operational budgeting.

There was no doubt that the Criminal Justice Commission invested a lot of money in the operation and, generally, that Joe and Jessie were properly looked after. At times Joe was given several hundred dollars to play poker machines alongside Lemberg (like Lemberg, he usually lost the money). But the social pressure that came from mixing with drug dealers and users, together with the constant need to keep up appearances, meant that Joe and Jessie frequently had to use their own money to maintain the illusion of having cash on tap.

Joe's and Jessie's authority to make operational decisions was often ambiguous. For an undercover cop, minimising risk was always the first priority. For a drug dealer it was usually profit. Opportunities outside the prearranged game plan (such as impromptu drug buys) and unexpected variations in quantity and price often resulted in the need to make excuses and create delays in order to seek permission to act from superiors. Most frustrating of all was Joe's inability—as a supposed big-time drug dealer—to supply even a single gram of cocaine or amphetamine to Detective Peter Reid. By demanding it, Reid succeeded in creating confusion and stress for Joe and his handlers in both Queensland and New South Wales. They all knew the risk to the operation (and potentially to Joe himself) if Joe was unable to supply the drug. The refusal by the Queensland authorities to allow Joe to play along—it was at the time prohibited by law—gave Reid a significant, if ephemeral, victory, but in the long run it didn't save Reid from conviction and a long jail sentence.

Then there was the checking of their covert identities on the police computer by corrupt police. Efficient operational planning had covered this contingency, but the risk of leaks within a corrupt police force meant that Joe's and Jessie's safety could never be guaranteed.

Joe's mood swings made matters worse. His steroid use exacerbated both his depression and his anger, and Jessie found it increasingly difficult to calm him. Both he and Jessie were well aware that they had not been receiving the psychological support that was supposed to be given to undercover operatives. In late 1999 they underwent some mandatory training and psychological testing in Brisbane and Sydney. While these tests found elevated levels of hostility and cynicism, their supervisor, Sergeant Pickering, reported: 'Welfare of the Undercover Operatives: Both fit and well and they are much more [sic] in a happier frame of mind than I anticipated. I will make sure that they are monitored and take any necessary action.' Joe and Jessie were dismissive of Pickering's assessment. 'Bullshit,' was their response.

For the next two months they spent most of their time preparing statements and finishing paperwork relating to

Craven. At the same time both sought in-house psychological
and personal support. They were restless and unsure of their
futures. But Joe and Jessie were not the only ones under
pressure. SCIA had its own worries, with major operational
and managerial shortcomings (including the undocumented
surveillance of senior police), human resource issues and
breaches of departmental policies and procedures. SCIA
would be seriously embarrassed if any of these became
known.

*

Around midday on Friday 3 March 2000 a Holden
Commodore containing several young Tongan men stopped
at traffic lights in Corrimal Street, Wollongong. A group
of young Lebanese men pulled up beside them in another
car. An argument followed and 22-year-old Fouad 'Fred'
Ekermawi, a passenger in the second car, fired at least ten
shots at the Commodore from a 9-millimetre semiautomatic
Browning pistol. A seventeen-year-old passenger in the
Commodore was wounded and two innocent pedestrians
were hit by pieces of shrapnel. Both cars drove off before the
police arrived.

Fouad was a menacing figure with a history of violence.
A fitness fanatic, he was 180 centimetres tall and weighed
110 kilograms. Six months earlier, without a gang behind
him, he had gone to Wollongong and told the 'coconuts'

[Tongans] that he was 'taking over' the distribution of cocaine in the area. The Tongans were not about to let a profitable drug run go without a fight. Threats were soon followed by violence. It was almost inevitable that someone was going to be killed.

The day after the shooting at the traffic lights, Fouad and others arrived at a friend's home in Berkeley, near Wollongong, and confronted a man who was accusing Fouad's friend of sleeping with his wife. A fight started and one of those with Fouad shouted, 'Pop him, pop him, just pop him.' Fouad pulled out a gun—the same gun he had used the day before—aimed it at the victim's head, then lowered the gun and fired three shots, hitting him in the left hand and left leg.

Within days police had information that the shooter in both incidents was Fouad. On 10 March Fouad rang Joe, whom he had known since childhood. He knew Joe as a former cop, kicked out of the police for corruption and now a drug dealer, muscleman and gangster. Fouad wanted help. 'He sounded anxious,' Joe recalls:

He asked if I could get him a magazine for a Browning 9 millimetre. I told him it shouldn't be difficult and asked him when he wanted it. 'Straightaway,' he told me. I asked him if there was anything the matter. I'd known Fouad a long time—we had gone to school together—and I had a fair idea of what he might be up to now. I wanted to help him if I could. At the same time I was an undercover cop. I had a role to play and I didn't want to do anything that would blow my cover. 'There's nothing the matter,' he said. 'I just need the clip.' I told him I ought to have one lying around. I said if I could find it I'd let him have it for nothing. I told him to call me the next day. I could see he was mixed up in something serious and I wanted to find a way out that didn't involve anyone getting shot. I knew it was risky to be talking guns with a guy like Fouad but I seriously believed I could handle it.

The next night Fouad rang. 'I haven't been able to find my clip,' Joe told him, 'but I got another 9-mill clip from a friend. You'll have to call around and see if it fits.' Fouad said that he would come over. When he arrived, Joe saw at once how agitated he was.

'What's going on?' Joe asked.

'Nothing,' said Fouad. 'Why?'

'You're acting weird, mate. Just tell me what's the matter.'

'I'm in a hurry. Show me the magazine.'

'I haven't got one,' said Joe. 'The guy didn't drop it off.'

'You fucking told me you had it,' shouted Fouad.

'Calm down. The guy is supposed to drop it off any time now. Just give it a few minutes.'

'I can't,' said Fouad, heading towards the front door. 'I have to go.'

Joe knew something was badly wrong but did not know what. He had not seen the Browning pistol Fouad claimed to have but he could see the state he was in and knew Fouad's capacity for violence. He tried to keep the conversation going.

'Mate, you've got to tell me what's going on. Do you need me to come with you?'

'It's nothing. I have some dramas and need the magazine and thought you could help.'

'I want to help. I'm just waiting for the guy. Tell me what's happening. Are you in trouble?'

'No, I'm fine. I just need the magazine. When your guy brings it, call me.'

Like every other police officer in Sydney, Joe was aware of the murderous feud between rival Lebanese youth gangs in the city's south-west. He knew that Fouad mixed with some gang members. It wasn't clear whether Fouad had committed a crime or whether he was being threatened by a gang, but Joe knew that the best thing for Fouad was to get him to go to the police of his own accord. The next day a friend called Joe and told him that Fouad had been arrested.

What Joe didn't know was that Fouad's telephone was being intercepted by police. They had picked up the conversations about the 9-millimetre magazine and Fouad had been under surveillance when he visited Joe. The police had also followed Fouad from Joe's home to Bankstown, where his parents lived. Fouad's parents' home had been kept under surveillance all night. The next morning officers from the heavily armed State Protection Group, together with negotiators and members of the State Protection Support Unit, called on Fouad to surrender. He attempted to escape but was arrested jumping a fence into a neighbour's property where police were waiting. He was carrying a loaded Browning pistol and 98 rounds of ammunition. Interviewed at Bankstown police station, Fouad made admissions about the two shootings (the Browning had been used in both) and was charged.

Fouad pleaded guilty. Fifteen months later, Wollongong Judge Joe Phelan took into consideration Fouad's immaturity and ordered him to enter the violent offenders' program whilst in custody. He was sentenced to nine years' jail. In 2006 Fouad was released on parole. However, it was not long before he was back in jail, charged with assaulting his wife. Fouad's parole over the Wollongong shootings was revoked when he pleaded guilty to the assault and he served out the rest of that sentence.

As a result of his meetings with Fouad, Joe became the focus of a major police investigation which also dragged in Jessie. The investigation was conducted by SCIA: a highly dubious arrangement given that Joe and Jessie had raised questions about the integrity of some SCIA investigations, and about its management and operational practices.

Since returning to Sydney Joe had been working out at the Body Sports gym in Louis Street, Granville, where he had trained since 1997. It was a way of relieving tension and forgetting his problems at SCIA. Many of those who trained there were of Middle Eastern background, but there was also a large group of Pacific Islanders. Joe was known as a former police officer turned drug dealer and bodyguard. At 155 kilograms he was the biggest person in the gym. 'I bench pressed 260 kilograms, leg pressed 800 kilograms and shoulder pressed 250 kilograms,' he recalls. 'I was taking steroids and testosterone. It wasn't a secret to anyone and I knew almost everyone at the gym.'

One morning Sergeant Pickering asked to see Joe. He told Joe that there was 'a gym job to be done'. It involved the sale of steroids and was going to be handled by Queensland undercover operatives who had been brought to Sydney for the job. Pickering asked Joe to speak with one of the operatives and 'give him a rundown on pricing and what's around to give him a heads up'. For some reason Pickering suggested he speak with the operative over the phone rather than meet him face to face.

Joe was puzzled. Why were they bringing in a Queenslander to do the job? Why shouldn't they meet face to face? Pickering gave Joe a mobile and a number to dial. Joe briefed the operative but the conversation left him more confused than ever. 'I was thinking the poor bastard had no idea what he was getting himself into. I also thought that the crook, whoever he was, was a lucky bastard. The u/c would have to pick up his game if he was to suck anyone in.'

Pickering asked Joe to bring in some sample vials of steroids to enable the operative to 'familiarise himself with the tools of the trade'. It seemed a strange request. 'A vial is a vial, whether you're in Sydney or Queensland,' Joe thought. 'This must be his first job.' Nevertheless, the next day he gave Pickering two empty vials. They were vials that Joe and Jessie had previously used when lecturing trainee undercover operatives.

Joe continued to train at the Granville gym. A few days after his last meeting with Pickering, a stranger turned up at the gym. Joe remembers him being Caucasian, in his mid-twenties, and unusually thin. 'He looked like someone who didn't belong in a gym, particularly this gym.' On the third day the new man approached Joe, commented on his size and asked Joe about his training habits. 'Then, out of the blue, he asked if I could give him any Methandrosteno-lone. I was shocked. This was the proper name for a powerful type of steroid. In all my years of training and undercover work I had never heard anyone call the drug by its medical name.'

'No,' Joe replied. 'Sorry, bro.'

But the man was persistent, 'Can you get me anything? I really want to get big.'

Again Joe told him he was unable to help, but the man wouldn't give up. He asked Joe if he could put him onto anyone 'who can get me the stuff'. Joe said he couldn't and advised the stranger to return when the gym was full and ask around.

The man kept pushing Joe for the name of a supplier. By now Joe knew he was up to something. The man was too pushy; he did not seem to know his way around the machines; and he'd chosen a gym where his was virtually the only Caucasian face. Furthermore, he arrived each day just after Joe, as though he had been waiting outside or had even been following him. Joe was certain about one thing: the stranger knew nothing about steroids. Some of the questions he was asking sounded very much like those Joe had been asked on the phone a few days earlier by the Queensland undercover cop. Before leaving the gym Joe offered the man some advice: 'Don't ask for Methandrostenolone,' he said. 'Call them pinkys or Dbols.'

The next day Joe went to see Pickering. He asked straightaway: 'Are you guys doing a job on me?'

Pickering was obviously taken aback. 'What are you talking about?' he asked.

Joe told him about the man at the gym and their conversation about steroids.

'You've been doing this work too long,' Pickering told him. 'You're paranoid.'

'If you guys are out to get me you'll need someone better than that. The bloke stuck out like dogs' balls.'

Pickering was right: Joe had been undercover for too long and he was paranoid. But Joe's hunch was correct. After the altercation with Pickering, the stranger stopped coming to the gym. Joe wondered what had happened to the two empty vials he had given Pickering for the Queensland cop. He soon found out.

Chapter 14
Charged

On 7 April 2000 Flemington police—probably acting on a tip-off from SCIA—telephoned Joe with some questions about his firearms licence. Joe had been a keen pistol shooter since before he joined the police. He owned several pistols and often went shooting at the practice range with colleagues. It turned out that Joe's licence had expired two years earlier but the weapons were still in his possession. As a result of the conversation Joe was asked to visit the police station and surrender the guns. There was no urgency in the request: when Joe said he was about to go away for a few days, he was given permission to leave the guns at his parents' home until he returned.

Ten days after the initial phone call, Joe went to Flemington police station and handed in four guns, together with his expired licence. He explained that he had been in Queensland on a major undercover operation and had forgotten to renew the licence, which he had held since 1991. Once again, Joe apologised for his mistake and promised to sort out the necessary paperwork and submit a renewal application in the next few days. The officer seemed satisfied and Joe assumed that was the end of the matter. If they had really been concerned, he thought, they would not have allowed him to leave the weapons with his parents before coming to the station.

There was still paperwork to be done for Operation Craven. After it was finished, Joe and Jessie were looking forward to a holiday together. Then out of the blue each received a telephone call from their supervisor, Sergeant Pickering, telling them to go to their safe house to complete their reports. Being told to do paperwork on a day off seemed an odd request, but both complied. Joe's unease was heightened by the news that SCIA now wanted to interview him about his expired firearms licence.

On the day Joe went to Internal Affairs, Jessie drove to Sydney's Star City Hotel in Darling Harbour to meet her sister, who had returned to Sydney after three years overseas. As she was parking her car, Jessie received a call on her mobile phone. It was from someone calling herself Detective Acting

Inspector Carole Dowsen. Jessie knew of someone at SCIA named Carole Dowsen, but her rank was senior constable, not detective acting inspector. The two weren't friends.

Dowsen told Jessie to report immediately to the SCIA office but Jessie refused, telling Dowsen that she was off duty and had arranged to meet her sister. 'Look,' Dowsen replied, 'we can do this the easy way or we can do it the hard way. I know you've just parked your car, you're at Star City in Darling Harbour ... I'm giving you fifteen minutes to get to the third floor of Internal Affairs.'

Jessie realised she was under surveillance. She could only interpret Dowsen's words as a threat. Dowsen wouldn't tell her why she had to go to SCIA but Jessie knew that if she was under surveillance it must be serious. She guessed that if she didn't do what she was told, she would probably be arrested anyway. Distressed and confused, Jessie broke down. She knew she had done nothing wrong but she was in no state to convince SCIA of her innocence. In Joe's absence the one person she could turn to was her sister. Ignoring the deadline, Jessie went to look for her. They didn't have long but with her sister's help Jessie managed to pull herself together to face Dowsen.

After arriving at SCIA, Jessie was taken to an interview room. Dowsen wasted no time in getting down to business: 'Your office is off, cars are off and Joe's phone's off, OK? [All had been bugged.] So let's just get started.' Jessie asked why she was there but Dowsen refused to answer. The signs, however, were ominous. During the taped interview Jessie was questioned about being an accessory before and after the fact to a homicide; about fraud; taking drugs and selling drugs. Frightened as she was, Jessie could see that the real target of the investigation wasn't her: it was Joe.

> *They were painting this crazy picture of Joe, who I'd known very closely for three years—they said he was selling drugs, supplying steroids and guns for homicides. All through the interview I was saying, 'No, no, you don't understand. During the Royal Commission Joe told everyone he quit the Police Service because he was corrupt. Everyone thought he was a big drug dealer, even his own family thought he was a drug dealer. That's what he was pretending to be. That's what you wanted him to be. But it wasn't real.*

Jessie was experienced enough to know that Dowsen was not doing things by the book but she felt too intimidated to fight back. She remembered conversations between her and Joe—several of which were over the telephone—in which they had lamented their poor treatment by police management.

At the end of the interview Jessie was allowed to leave. As a parting shot, Dowsen encouraged her to 'have a holiday' while the investigation into Joe's activities was under way. As she left SCIA, she saw Joe in an interview room, but they were not allowed to speak. It was obvious to her that he was under arrest.

As soon as she was outside, Jessie rang Joe's parents. Joe's mother was hysterical. Heavily armed police in bulletproof vests were searching the house and there was a helicopter circling overhead. There was nothing Jessie could do, no one she could call. 'Just cooperate with them,' Jessie told her.

It was perhaps fortunate for Joe that he was unaware of what was happening at his parents' home. After leaving the safe house, Joe had driven to Internal Affairs, arriving about 1 pm. He was immediately questioned about his expired firearms licence and his possession of four handguns covered by the licence. The investigation was being conducted as an internal police inquiry.

Joe was also interviewed over his connection with Fouad. In particular he was questioned about the telephone conversation during which he had appeared to offer Fouad an ammunition clip. Joe explained that since Fouad did not know he was an undercover police officer, he'd had no choice but to play along in order to protect his cover. Joe had nothing to hide and made no attempt to conceal anything. But in some of his answers he made mistakes about times and dates. Sometimes he was confused about the sequence of conversations. On top of this, Joe had seen Jessie walk past, escorted by two police, during a break in the interview. He could see that she had been crying and had tried in vain to talk to her through the glass window. Not knowing what was happening to Jessie only made Joe more desperate.

In the minds of his interviewers each mistake, each misremembered conversation, was further evidence against Joe. The more he said, the more he incriminated himself. Without knowing it, Joe was slowly digging himself into a hole from which he could not escape.

During the interview Joe was shown two empty vials of steroids. He recognised them as being the two vials he had given to Pickering a couple of weeks earlier for the Queensland undercover cops. They were vials he had kept from his days in the drug squad for use in other jobs—why were they being shown to him now? They were left provocatively on the table. No questions were asked.

Later that afternoon SCIA Inspector Antonjuk informed Joe that a search warrant had been executed on his parents' home and, as a result of property found in his bedroom, it was now a criminal investigation. He told Joe, 'You are under arrest in relation to the possession of unlicensed firearms and [in] respect of prescribed restricted substances and what is believed to be prohibited drugs.' Cautioned that he need not answer any further questions, Joe refused to say any more.

Joe was taken to the City Central police station. Two hours later he was charged by SCIA with several firearms and drug offences. As the charges were being processed, Jessie received a telephone call from Detective Sergeant Deborah Wallace of SCIA. Wallace told Jessie that Joe had been arrested and taken to City Central. As Jessie and her sister waited outside the police station, Detectives Antonjuk and Wallace came outside to explain the charges. Jessie did her best to defend Joe but she was too bewildered to understand the accusations against him. This was Joe they were talking about, not some drug-dealing gangster. Jessie was conscious of the irony of standing there with Wallace, the SCIA officer she had been assigned to target eighteen months earlier for alleged (but unfounded) 'inappropriate associations'. (Wallace would not learn of the operation for almost another two years.)

Joe was finally released from the police station around 9.30 pm that evening. He was, in Jessie's words, 'a fucking mess'. Jessie and her sister went to meet him, hoping to be able to 'calm him down' with a couple of drinks. But it was immediately obvious that, in Joe's overwrought state, alcohol would only make things worse. After one drink they all drove home.

Neither Joe nor Jessie got much sleep that night. The next morning, as they struggled to make sense of what had happened, Joe suddenly announced: 'I've got two more guns that they didn't even find.'

Jessie was stunned. 'Where?'

Joe pointed to a cardboard shoe box on the bed. Inside were a 357 Smith and Wesson revolver and a .22 calibre Victor target pistol. When the police arrived to search the house, the box had been lying under a pile of blankets on top of the bedroom cupboard. How could they have missed it? The possibility suddenly dawned on him that he was being set up. What if the police raided the house a second time and found the two guns? They could easily accuse him of having obtained more guns since the first raid.

Even if it was a cock-up rather than a conspiracy, the guns represented a big problem for Joe. They had belonged to Joe's uncle who had surrendered them to police three years earlier. Joe had then bought them from his uncle and lawfully retrieved them from the police. On 1 May, after taking legal advice, Joe went to the Flemington police station and surrendered both guns. A few days later Joe was suspended from duty on full pay.

During the next two months further charges were laid against Joe. There were now 37 charges including six counts of using an unauthorised firearm; seven counts of not ensuring safekeeping of a firearm (both the using and not ensuring safekeeping charges included the two firearms that had been missed by the police in their search and handed in by Joe); one count of unauthorised possession of a firearm; one count of possessing ammunition, and four counts of possessing prohibited weapons (knives); fourteen counts of possessing prescribed restricted substances (steroids) and four counts of possessing a prohibited drug—cocaine (0.42 grams), ecstasy (0.24 grams), speed (0.59 grams) and cannabis (0.4 grams).

A few days after Joe's arrest, Jessie went to their Sydney safe house to collect some personal belongings, but the locks had been changed. The final insult came a couple of days later, when Jessie received a telephone call from an officer at SCIA asking why she was not at work. When she demanded to know whether she was still under investigation, Jessie got no answer. Instead of going back to work Jessie went on sick leave due to stress and did not return to active duty for another seven months.

As for Joe, he remembers feeling as though he'd been 'raped' by the police hierarchy. In truth, Joe found himself the fall-guy in an internecine battle within the New South Wales Police. By appearing to help a violent criminal like Fouad Ekermawi, Joe had made himself vulnerable to the accusation that, as an undercover cop, he really was the gangster he was pretending to be. Joe's bosses at SCIA saw at once that if Joe was on trial, so was SCIA. After all, SCIA was the organisation responsible for upholding integrity within the police. Now it was being accused, through Joe, of colluding with organised crime. Its own management practices and operational procedures were in the firing line. In the views of SCIA command, the only way the organisation could vindicate itself was by taking the lead in investigating and prosecuting Joe, despite the flagrant conflict of interest involved. No other command would have been allowed to carry out an investigation of what looked like serious corruption in its own ranks. By investigating Joe, SCIA was flouting the very principle of impartiality it was created to protect. Arrested at gunpoint, searched for concealed weapons and accused of being a drug dealer, Joe could identify for the first time with fellow Muslims who complained of being hounded and persecuted by the police simply for being Muslims. 'It made me think they saw all of us as Telopea Street Boys,' he says, referring to the notorious Lebanese street gang that terrorised south-west Sydney during the late 1990s and early 2000s. 'They thought we were all the same.'

As a uniformed officer, Joe had felt respected both by his colleagues on the streets and by the police hierarchy. The trouble had begun for him the day someone decided that his background and colour would make him useful as an undercover cop. Looking back, Joe realised it was then that his sense of himself had started to unravel. As an undercover cop he no longer had the sure identity he'd had while in uniform. His new job meant publicly repudiating everything he'd joined the police to uphold. Nor, Joe quickly discovered, could he count on the reassurance and support of senior colleagues. He and Jessie were thrown back entirely on each other. When there were problems, they had no one else to turn to. Worse, many of those problems were caused not by the criminals he was supposed to be targeting, but by his own superiors. To Joe, the ethnic background that had once been so valued was now a liability. It was a sign of Joe's mounting paranoia that he found it easier to identify with his criminal targets than with his colleagues in the police. Would he have been treated like this, he wondered, if he hadn't been a Muslim?

Chapter 15
Shame

As well as the anguish he was suffering on his own account, Joe was tormented by the distress he had caused his parents. While both knew he was innocent and stood by him, they were devastated by the disgrace they had to bear among their extended family and friends in the local community. Until now they had been able to bear any public shame in the knowledge that their eldest son had been putting his life at risk in order to make the streets safer for everyone. It was a story that would one day make the Lebanese community proud, they told themselves. Suddenly that inner comfort and belief had been shattered. To Joe, he had let down his parents and the community: he was responsible for the pain they were suffering. He felt he had lost everything. 'I was shell shocked,' Joe recalls:

It took a week for me just to understand the charges. They weren't pretend charges against a pretend gangster. They were real charges and their object was to send me to jail. I knew I'd done nothing wrong but nobody would listen to me. They had already made up their minds. I took a fistful of tablets and went to sleep. I don't know if I wanted to kill myself. I was in the same position as the drunks and junkies I'd met on the streets of Kings Cross. Taking those pills was the only way I could think of to escape.

The tablets Joe took had been prescribed to help him manage stress and depression. About an hour later Jessie found him unconscious in his bed at his parents' home. Unable to lift or even support him because of his size, Jessie and Joe's parents struggled to get him to sit up. After several minutes of being slapped and splashed with water Joe vomited and regained consciousness. He was dazed and didn't know where he was. Jessie had called an ambulance but when the officers tried to help, Joe became aggressive. After finally managing to pacify him, they took him to Auburn Hospital, where Joe was admitted and treated before being released the next day into the care of his parents.

Within weeks of his arrest, Joe's story was leaked to the media. On 10 May the *Sydney Morning Herald* published a story headlined 'Drug arrest of undercover officer':

'An undercover detective investigating crooked police in Sydney's heartland of drug trafficking and gang warfare has been arrested and charged with firearm and drug offences ... The detective, from the elite Special Crime and Internal Affairs unit, the most secretive in the NSW Police Service, was allegedly seduced by the underworld lifestyle he was forced to live.' The reporter, Les Kennedy, went on to note that 'His [the detective's] arrest has created fears that other investigations into the possible links between organised crime and crooked police might have been compromised.' The arrest was described as 'a major embarrassment for the Police Commissioner, Mr Peter Ryan, and Assistant Commissioner, Mr Mal Brammer, commander of Internal Affairs'.

The same day the police media unit issued a statement entitled 'Police Refute Claims of Arrest Cover Up' which quoted Deputy Commissioner Moroney as saying he had 'asked South Eastern Region Commander Christine Nixon late last year [at least five months earlier and well before Joe's arrest] to conduct an internal review of undercover policing'. Nixon later gave a different account. 'In April 2000,' she wrote, 'I was requested by Deputy Commissioner Moroney to undertake a comprehensive review of the operations of the Undercover Branch.' This was only a matter of weeks earlier and one month after Joe's arrest. It was a significant contradiction.

Kennedy followed up his story with another the next day. Under the headline 'Police Fear for Inquiries', Kennedy wrote: 'Undercover police operations involving an Internal Affairs officer charged with drug and firearms offences are being reviewed amid fears that some cases may have been compromised ... The Special Operations Commander, Deputy Commissioner Ken Moroney, also indicated the review was examining the screening of officers chosen to infiltrate major organised crime networks or suspected corrupt police rings.'

Two days later a third article, by Phil Cornford and Les Kennedy, described the ramifications for the police of 'a strategically placed NSW undercover police officer [who] may have gone bad'. The repercussions of his arrest, they wrote, had been 'traumatic at the Clarence Street headquarters of the Special Crime and Internal Affairs branch, the "cop busters", the most secretive—and usually the most secure—agency in the NSW Police Service'.

According to Cornford and Kennedy, the anonymous officer's arrest jeopardised 'not only operations which are aimed at penetrating to the core of organised crime and their corrupt police protectors but the lives of other undercover operatives'. They noted that at the time of the arrest 'police were conducting a major campaign following about 40 shooting incidents, including a drive-by fusillade at Lakemba police station, a gunfight with police, and a number of murders'.

Joe and Jessie were horrified by the media coverage, which they believed was part of a conspiracy by police

management. There were serious mistakes in the *Herald*'s
reports which could only have been supplied by the police,
with the deliberate intention, they thought, of endangering
their lives. For instance, the implication that Joe was
involved in the investigation of the '40 shooting incidents'
was untrue. Neither Joe nor Jessie, nor SCIA for that matter,
had anything to do with investigating the shootings, which
was the job of Crime Agencies, the forerunner to State Crime
Command.

Joe was told by a SCIA officer that the story had been
leaked by Assistant Commissioner Clive Small (co-author of
this book) and by then Detective Superintendent Nick Kaldas,
but this was impossible, since the media leaks contained
information known only to those close to the investigation
of Joe, either in SCIA or the Police Executive.

Joe was now having constant medical treatment. Over
the next two years there would be nearly a hundred visits to
doctors, psychologists and psychiatrists. Joe was diagnosed
as suffering paranoia, stress, depression, adjustment disorders
and anxiety. He depended on a cocktail of powerful
prescription drugs. Crucially, he was now having difficulty
separating himself from his undercover life, telling one of his
doctors that he was 'currently Robbie the bodyguard'. Joe
also had to make several trips to Brisbane to testify in court
hearings relating to Operation Craven. Throughout this time
Jessie was always at his side. But Jessie had problems of her

own. While she was not facing criminal charges, her own police career seemed over. In 2000 Jessie was diagnosed with severe depression and anxiety, including panic attacks. Doctors classified her illnesses as work-related.

Joe had taken steroids for four and a half years. They had given him the confidence and physical strength he needed to survive in the underworld. Now he had given them up, but the consequences were severe. He lost fitness and muscle tone. The psychological strain of coming off steroids was compounded by his other problems and by the medication he was taking, but he managed to stay away from them for nearly a year.

But in mid-2000 Joe's behaviour attracted the attention of local police. About 5 pm on 11 July Joe and two others—both of Lebanese background—were seen in a car by security officers in Holker Road, Silverwater, in western Sydney. The location made the security officers suspicious: it was not far from the Nike Hospitality Facility, Newington Business Park, the Silverwater Correctional Centre and the Olympic Village. Were the three men targeting the business park for a robbery, organising a break-out from the low-security correctional centre, or planning a terrorist attack on the Olympics? Or were they, like thousands of others, simply having an innocent look at the Olympic site?

The security officers had reason to be wary: in 2000 a wave of violent crime was being committed across south and south-west Sydney by men of Middle Eastern appearance; the risk of terrorism against the Olympic Games was considered to be very high, and the threat of a jail break-out was ever-present. Neither Joe nor his passengers was spoken to but the security officers reported the suspicious sighting to police, who circulated the incident through the police network.

It was now several months since their return from Queensland, but Jessie was still having trouble leasing an apartment. Because she had been living under false names for two years, she had no recent credit history or references under her proper name and no landlord would give her a lease. To the real estate agents Jessie was literally a woman with no past.

Around the time Joe was being reported for acting suspiciously around the Olympic site, he and Jessie started looking at apartments on the Pyrmont peninsula. One day Joe bumped into Tom Domican. It had been more than a year since they had seen one another. They had coffee and a general talk about what they had been doing. Joe explained that he and Jessie had been in Queensland 'doing their best' and that Jessie had been trying to rent an apartment in the area but kept being turned down because she did not have a credit history.

Without hesitating, Domican said, 'You're going to pay your rent and not dud me, are you? I'll fix it up and guarantee you,' said Domican. 'But I don't expect any trouble.'

Domican took Joe and Jessie to a nearby real estate office where he knew the agent. Jessie got her apartment. As Tom left, he said to Joe and Jessie, 'You owe me one.'

The irony was inescapable. Joe had tried to lock Domican up. He'd lied to him and pretended to be a friend, yet in half an hour Domican had done more to help him and Jessie than the police had done in years.

Joe was still unaware of the Silverwater police report when on the evening of 15 August police saw him and Jessie parked in their car in Pirrama Road, on the Pyrmont peninsula. About half an hour later the police again drove past and saw Joe and Jessie still in the car. They carried out a radio check of the car and were told that the 'occupants of this vehicle may be in possession of concealed firearms'.

Unfortunately for Joe and Jessie, they had parked in a street overlooking an area of the harbour where the Australian Army's Special Air Service Regiment, the New South Wales Police State Protection Group and the Water Police were conducting joint training exercises as part of Olympic security preparations. The police approached the car with caution. Joe was uncooperative and aggressive. To him, it was another case of being picked on.

A further radio check by the police in the squad car revealed that Joe had been the subject of other 'Olympic-related intelligence'—a reference to the Silverwater incident. Asked to explain what he was doing, Joe lost his temper and unwisely told the police that he had seen 'all the police activity in the Water Police Compound'. An inspection of the vehicle revealed that Joe was a police officer: the searcher found his Police Credit Union card. There were angry exchanges but eventually the police left. The incident provided material for yet another damaging report against Joe.

Joe did not tell police why he and Jessie were parked in Pirrama Road. They were both upset after an argument and were sitting in the car trying to sort things out when the police turned up. As for the Silverwater incident: 'All they had to do was ask me what we were doing. We just went there to have a look. We used to go there every couple of months to see what was happening. They could have asked me but they didn't.' In truth, simply asking Joe why he was there might not have done any good. As his behaviour on 15 August demonstrated, Joe's sense of injustice made him hostile to the police. It took little to turn that hostility into violence, either against them or himself.

With the Queensland court hearings just weeks away, Joe was drinking with two friends at Dancers Cabaret in Bayswater Road, Kings Cross, when he noticed two men talking at the bar. He instantly recognised one of them as Peter Reid. 'Somehow I managed to carry on as if nothing had happened,' Joe remembers, 'although inside I was in complete shock. The CJC had told me that Reid was on bail, but they had assured me that his bail conditions prevented him from leaving Queensland. But there he was, watching as if he thought he knew me but wasn't quite sure. I had changed my appearance since I had seen him last in February. Although I still wore flashy clothes, earrings and a goatie, I had gained fifteen kilos since Operation Craven, my long braids had been shaved off and I was bald. After staring at me for about half an hour Reid came over to where I was sitting. He said, 'Are you Joe?'

'No,' I answered. 'Why?'

'Have you ever gone by the name Joe?'

'No, mate,' I told him. 'My name is Robbie. Do I know you?'

Reid said, 'It's just that you look like this guy I know. Doesn't matter. Have a good night.'

'No problem,' I said. 'You too, bro.'

Reid gave me a long stare and then went back to his friend.

Jessie was on sick leave until November 2000 when she was classified as 'completely recovered' and fit for work. She immediately began training as a crime scene investigator in Forensic Services. But her recovery proved to be temporary. In late December a dispute with her flatmate over unpaid rent and other matters resulted in the police issuing a temporary restraining order against Jessie. The next day Jessie was stood down from Forensic Services. Her flatmate took out an Apprehended Violence Order against her. Jessie was interviewed by SCIA over the order, only for it to be withdrawn three weeks later at the next court appearance. The former flatmate said that she had felt pressured by the police into taking out the order.

Again Jessie returned to work, this time at the Child Protection Enforcement Agency (CPEA), Crime Agencies. She received strong support from the then commander of the CPEA, Superintendent John Heslop. 'He really helped me,' Jessie recalled. 'He was about the only senior police officer who ever did.'

Jessie soon found herself working on Operation Paradox, the largest community awareness campaign against child sexual abuse in Australia, run jointly by the New South Wales Police and the Department of Community Services. Months later Assistant Commissioner Graeme Morgan, the head of Crime Agencies, wrote this about Jessie's participation: 'All staff performed their duties with absolute professionalism. I believe however, that a great deal of that success can be attributed to the outstanding efforts and dedication of Senior Constable [Jessie]. I believe that she is deserving of recognition for those efforts.'

Superintendent Heslop agreed with Assistant Commissioner Morgan's assessment, and went further. 'I cannot but sing the praises of this Officer,' he wrote. 'She is extremely talented and skilled at negotiation, writing, developing plans, etc. She had no experience in this area of policing prior to her beginning [at] this Command. Her efforts were over and above what was expected. I highly recommend her to you for Commendation.'

Jessie received a Crime Agencies commander's commendation for 'outstanding performance and leadership demonstrated in the coordination of Operation Paradox'. She was formally transferred to a Child Protection Agency Joint Investigation Response Team and for the next two years served in Sydney's inner city and western suburbs. 'It was important work in Child Protection,' Jessie recalls:

They were good people to work with. They were very different to the people we worked with in Internal Affairs. I felt as though I was achieving something, but my mood still went up and down. I would have a three-month period where I felt good about myself and then I would fall back into a deep depression. But things were terrible for Joe. His whole world had collapsed—his career, his self-respect, his faith in the law, everything. A couple of times I thought he was close to suicide.

Chapter 16
Unprotected witness

The start of court hearings relating to Craven could not have come at a worse time for Joe. If his own legal problems weren't serious enough, he now had to stand up in front of the crooked cops who blamed him for the long jail sentences they were facing. If he was paranoid about his bosses at SCIA, Joe had every reason to fear the vengeance of men like Reid.

In December 2000 Jessie accompanied Joe to Brisbane, where they were met by Witness Protection and taken to a hotel. Joe was required to sign the usual protection agreement that included not telling anyone of their whereabouts, not making telephone calls and not contacting the media. The next morning Witness Protection took Joe to the Brisbane Magistrates Court to meet the prosecutor.

The meeting didn't go well. The prosecutor was aware of the charges Joe was facing in Sydney and seemed reluctant to answer his questions. Inevitably, Joe took this to mean the prosecutor didn't trust him. It would have been remarkable if the prosecutor had trusted him, since everything he and the Queensland Criminal Justice Commission knew about Joe had been fed to them by SCIA.

When the time came for him to take the witness stand against detectives Peter Reid, Gerry McArthur and Gregory Catton, Joe looked straight at Reid. As soon as Reid saw Joe he shook his head and gave a sly smile, realising at that moment that it had been Joe he had confronted at Dancers Cabaret.

Before he gave his evidence, Joe's real name was disclosed to the defence: at the time there was no provision in Queensland law to prevent this. (The law has since been changed.) The prosecutor began by asking him about the charges he faced back in Sydney:

'Is it true that you're a New South Wales policeman?'

'Yes,' Joe replied.

'Is it true that you've recently been charged with offences?'

'Yes.'

'Can you tell us what you've been charged with?'

'Firearms, steroids, weapons.'

'Are you still a police officer?'

'Yes.'

'Are you suspended?'

'Yes.'

'No further questions.'

While he knew the prosecutor had no choice but to ask these questions (if he hadn't asked them himself, the defence certainly would, with potentially far more damage to the Crown's case), Joe had been dreading them. Rather than the prosecution's chief witness, they made him feel like the defendant.

Not surprisingly, the defence tried to use Joe's admissions to discredit his evidence. Joe was questioned in detail about his medication. When he refused to answer some of the questions, the magistrate threatened him with a charge of contempt. The defence was delighted. The court was adjourned while Joe took advice from his Sydney lawyers. He re-entered the witness box and answered all the questions asked of him, but was unable to remember many details of the operation due to his medication and mental condition.

The next morning, 13 December, in an article headlined 'Corruption case key witness on drug counts', Simon Lomax of Brisbane's *Courier Mail* wrote: 'The case against two allegedly corrupt detectives suffered a major blow yesterday after it was revealed the CJC operative who collected most of the evidence had himself been charged with more than 30 drug and firearm offences.'

The same day, Joe re-entered the witness box and completed his evidence. After the court adjourned he returned immediately to Sydney for psychiatric treatment. The experience had been traumatic. The defence, however, had failed in its attempt to destroy Joe as a witness. McArthur, Catton and Reid were all committed for trial.

*

Both Joe and Jessie had kept their police-issue handguns when they went to Queensland to work on Craven, but when Craven ended in February 2000 they had given them to a colleague who was driving to Sydney. After returning to Sydney, neither Joe nor Jessie had been reissued with their guns. The failure of the police to return their weapons, without explanation, increased their sense of vulnerability.

A few months after giving evidence in Brisbane Joe was pulled over by police at Bass Hill in Sydney's south-west for speeding. Seeing Joe's agitated state, the police carried out checks over the radio and were told he had 'priors to assault police and has access to firearms'. They called for back-up. Joe's car, a 1980s classic American convertible, was searched and 'a black woollen balaclava, a black woollen beanie and a miniature baseball bat made of aluminium' were found on the floor behind the passenger's seat. Joe admitted that the property was his and told police the 'balaclava', as police described it, was to keep his head warm and the bat was 'to play baseball with'.

The police did not believe him and told Joe they intended to take the balaclava and bat and make further inquiries. Joe refused to sign the police notebook as a receipt for the items taken from him.

Bizarrely, it was not until later that the investigating police learned that Joe was a police officer. Reflecting on the incident, Joe now admits that his uncooperative behaviour only aggravated the situation and that, in part, he lied to them. The bat had been there for his protection—Reid and McArthur weren't the only criminals who had made threats against him—but the so-called 'balaclava' really was a beanie that he sometimes wore when driving. 'That bat caused me a lot of trouble but I really thought if I didn't take precautions the police weren't going to look after me. The risks you face as an undercover cop don't go away just because you have stopped working undercover. I'd had one contract taken out against my life and for all I knew there could have been others. The bat wasn't much but at least it was something I could use to defend myself.'

Chapter 17
Dismissal

The charges against Joe were finally heard at the Downing Centre Local Court on 19 March 2001. Those relating to possessing cocaine, ecstasy, methylamphetamine and cannabis were withdrawn by the Office of Public Prosecutions. Joe pleaded guilty to the remaining charges relating to firearms, prohibited weapons and possession of restricted substances, arguing mitigating circumstances. The magistrate adjourned the matter for a decision. Two weeks later, as a result of Joe's guilty pleas, then Deputy Commissioner Ken Moroney changed the status of Joe's suspension: from with pay to without pay.

As Joe waited for the magistrate's decision, he and his family suffered a further blow: his younger brother was charged with armed robbery in company. He later pleaded guilty and served almost three years' jail. Joe blamed himself for letting his brother go off the rails: 'It was my fault. I was schmoozing around thinking I was this bigshot drug dealer, hitman and crim and I never thought how it would affect my brother. He looked up to me. In his eyes I was some kind of hero. He copied what he saw and I was never able to tell him the truth.'

Joe made it his business to find the money to pay his brother's legal fees, explaining that 'in Arabic culture the first boy takes responsibility for all his siblings'. It would not be the last run-in Joe's brother would have with the law. In 2007, a year after his release from jail, his brother was again arrested and charged over a violent home invasion. Bail was refused. He eventually pleaded guilty to a lesser charge of assault occasioning actual bodily harm and was sentenced to eighteen months' jail.

With his brother in jail for armed robbery, Joe appeared at the Local Court on 18 May 2001. The magistrate, Mary Jerram, found the offences proven but recorded a conviction for one matter only: the unauthorised possession of a firearm (a gun was found under his bed). She placed Joe on a two-year good behaviour bond and imposed another two-year bond for his possession of steroids, with no conviction recorded. Explaining her decision, Magistrate Jerram told the court:

I don't think that anyone who has heard this evidence would quibble that it is a difficult matter for sentencing, and I want Mr Harris [the name given to Joe during the hearing] to hear me in saying that I think everybody would feel considerable compassion [for] him ... I've no doubt from what I've heard today, that it was the work itself which turned a cheerful, likeable—perhaps I could quote Sergeant Tannous's words, very pleasant, friendly, hard-working honest young man—into the rather sad person that I see before me today. Sad, of course, because of what's happened to him.

Accepting submissions made by lawyers on Joe's behalf, the magistrate observed that Joe:

was a young man who got to a point of having been involved in such dangerous work and essentially, what I've heard, changing his personality virtually as a result, and he believed ... that he and his family were under threat ... [and] that protection, of both himself and his family, was needed ... [Joe] didn't succumb to temptation in the sense he took to stealing or dealing in drugs ... [but] he took on the persona of the sort of persons he was dealing with by using the steroids and the gun collection was becoming frightening.

Joe did not escape reproach, the magistrate declaring that his possession of the unlicensed firearms 'far exceeded what may have been ordinary precautions' and that he had 'lost control of himself badly.' But her harshest criticism was for the police hierarchy. She noted that Joe 'wasn't, apparently, sufficiently reviewed and supervised psychologically or even perhaps by members of the service. And for somebody of his age in that sort of work ... [it] doesn't seem to have been sufficient or appropriate.' She had already acknowledged Joe's personal vulnerability and the very difficult and dangerous circumstances under which he operated, as well as the sincerity of his belief that his family was in danger.

Six months later, in November 2001, Joe read a report in the *Sydney Morning Herald* about an incident involving Police Commissioner Peter Ryan. According to the report, Ryan and his wife had arrived home one evening after a night out with their neighbours when they heard the sound of an intruder coming from the neighbours' home. 'The commissioner sent his wife, Adrienne, home to fetch his gun,' the paper told its readers. Startled police who had been called to the scene arrived 'to see a woman brandishing a handgun approaching a group of civilians and the NSW Police Commissioner'. The police quickly realised who was involved and turned their attention to 'whatever was going on inside the house'. A thorough search of the property revealed that the intruder was a possum. In the light of his own prosecution, Joe couldn't help wondering why no action was taken against Commissioner Ryan for (apparently) having an unsecured weapon in his house, or against Mrs Ryan for handling her husband's gun without a licence of her own.

With the criminal charges against him either withdrawn or dealt with, Joe could at last look forward to a semblance of normal life, although his future in the police service still hung in the balance. But within weeks another ghost from his undercover past came back to haunt him. The trial of John Visser on drug supply charges was set down for hearing in mid-2001. Visser had been arrested four years earlier at Summer Hill in Sydney's inner west in a sting set up by Joe while he was working for the Drug Enforcement Agency. The alleged $100,000 contract for a hit on Joe was still on offer. Joe had never forgotten Visser and his knowledge of the contract against him was one of Joe's reasons for keeping guns close by. In his volatile state, the pressure of having to testify against Visser was too much for Joe and his psychiatrist certified him unfit to give evidence. Visser beat the charges.

Meanwhile there were several in the police hierarchy who were far from happy with Joe's court result. Having started out with 35 criminal charges, they had seen a criminal conviction recorded for just a single matter. An appeal against the decision was considered before the idea was quashed by the Director of Public Prosecutions. Still looking for ways to punish Joe, the New South Wales Police then prepared a 181D loss of commissioner's confidence dismissal notice. (Loss of commissioner's confidence notices were introduced after the 1994–97 Wood Royal Commission into the New South Wales Police Service. Their purpose was to enable the commissioner to remove police officers 'if the Commissioner did not have confidence in the police officer's suitability to continue as a police officer, having regard to the police officer's competence, integrity, performance or conduct'.) The basis of the dismissal notice was to be the criminal charges that had already been dealt with by Magistrate Jerram. Assistant Commissioner Mal Brammer, the former head of Internal Affairs, was asked for his opinion about the proposal to dismiss Joe. Brammer wrote:

The Officer [Joe] performed some very difficult and risky tasks in this Command with apparent professionalism pursuing corruption. In particular his intrinsic undercover role in the exposure of corruption in the Queensland Police Service on behalf of the Criminal Justice System is to be highly commended.

Unfortunately his serious and criminal behaviour in his private life has severely discounted against those achievements in breaching the ideals of this Service, this Command and those who supervised and supported him in his endeavours.

Whilst the processes leading to his engagement in this Command could have been better, the officer can only hold himself to account for his present and tenuous position. I can offer no mitigation that would support his continuance as a member of the Service.

Disregarding Magistrate Jerram's strong criticism of SCIA's performance, Brammer accepted no responsibility for Joe's predicament, either as the commander of SCIA or, before that, as a senior officer in the Drug Enforcement Agency. Brammer's comment that 'the processes leading to [Joe's] engagement in this Command could have been better' grossly understated management shortcomings that were, by then, well known not just to Brammer himself and senior officers in SCIA, but to Commissioner Ryan and at least some others in the police hierarchy. They should also have been known to Ken Moroney. As the deputy commissioner (Special Operations) from mid-1999 until his appointment as commissioner in 2002, Moroney had been directly responsible for SCIA.

Procedural fairness required that Joe be given an opportunity to respond to the commissioner's decision before the notice took effect. Joe did not shirk responsibility either for his use of steroids or for his possession of the firearms, but he tried to explain the circumstances surrounding both.

Certainly there was a personal benefit to my use of steroids and I do not seek to walk away from that. However, there was also a considerable component of my use which is related, if not attributable, to my duties as a police officer ... It would have been impossible for me to maintain my cover by being a 'gym junkie' without the use of steroids to assist me to train ... the steroids found in my premises were for my personal use and at no time did I participate in the sale of those drugs to any person ... The firearm located under my bed during the execution of the search warrant [the offence for which a conviction was recorded] ... was there for my personal protection ... Since my return from Queensland I have been particularly concerned about my safety and had not been provided with a firearm by the Police Service.

Joe mentioned his fear of John Visser, whose long history of violence, including the attempted murder of a former accomplice and his two young children in a car bombing, should have been enough to convince SCIA that Joe and Jessie needed protection. He also explained how he came to possess the resealable plastic bags containing minute traces of cocaine, ecstasy, amphetamines and cannabis. This was the first time Joe had mentioned the drugs, since he had declined to answer questions at the time of his arrest and the Director of Public Prosecutions had subsequently dropped the charges. The bags containing traces of drugs, Joe said, had come from the police themselves, together with other empty bags. 'I was not knowingly in possession of those drugs ... [they] ... were obtained by me from the Police Service (particularly the Drug Enforcement Agency and Special Services Group undercover units), as were the other plastic bags, for use in my undercover work and for lectures to undercover police.'

Some colleagues at SCIA had been attached to the drug squad that had supplied Joe with the drug bags and these very officers had been involved in the investigation that saw him charged with possession of those bags—a procedural abuse that should have alerted senior police to the systemic flaws within SCIA. But it was Joe who was on trial, not SCIA, and Brammer's view that Joe should be dismissed prevailed. In late October 2001 Commissioner Ryan signed the commissioner's loss of confidence notice and Joe was formally removed from the police.

For Joe, this was the final betrayal by the police and a severe personal humiliation. He went on an alcohol binge (as one of his psychiatrists put it, he 'self-medicated with alcohol'). In Joe's words, 'I was so down that I wanted to kill myself. I thought my life was over and there was nothing I could do to redeem myself.'

A few days later Joe received a telephone call from Jennifer Lette, the police psychologist appointed to check on his welfare. When he answered the call Joe was heavily affected by alcohol and antidepressant drugs. Angry and aggressive, he talked about the shame he'd brought on his family and the need to regain his dignity. Joe rambled and talked about killing the senior police he held responsible for destroying his career. 'I'm going to the Avery Building … If I get the chance to speak to him [the commissioner] then that's a different story.' The psychologist rang Joe's psychiatrist, Dr Murray Wright, who immediately rang Joe and assessed him to be 'a dangerous person in his current mood'. The commissioner and police headquarters were put on alert.

Joe was standing outside the Avery Building, drunk and abusive, when Jennifer Lette arrived. He entered the foyer area but was refused entry—Peter Ryan had no intention of meeting him. After a while he was coaxed outside by Lette and Roz Garbutt, a police psychologist. Eventually Joe agreed to leave. He was in no condition to drive so at his request Lette and Garbutt took him to Kings Cross. After dropping him they alerted the duty officer at Kings Cross police station, fearing that Joe would get himself into trouble.

Joe spent the afternoon wandering the streets and alleys of Kings Cross. As night fell he visited some of the nightclubs where he had spent much of his time just a few years earlier. Around midnight Jessie picked him up and took him home. Years later Joe reflected, 'I can't remember much about that day. I don't know why I went to the Cross. All I know is that I had completely lost it and wanted to go somewhere where I could get some respect. I thought I'd get respect in the Cross, even if it was from gangsters, but when I got there it was different. Nobody gave a fuck. I was nobody.'

The following morning, 6 November, Joe was again seen sitting in the park across the road from police headquarters. Once again, he was dosed up with alcohol and antidepressant drugs. A short time earlier Joe had attempted to enter police headquarters but after being told the commissioner would not see him, he left without argument. Again, Jennifer Lette was called. This time Joe was calm. After she spoke with him, Joe went home.

For the third day in a row Joe went to police headquarters demanding to see the commissioner. Again, Joe had been drinking heavily and left without seeing Ryan.

A day or two later Joe telephoned Jennifer Lette and told her he no longer had any desire to meet the commissioner. Instead he would be taking his complaints to the courts. Joe knew he had done the wrong thing by making threats and trying to force the commissioner to see him. 'I was frustrated and all avenues [within the police] had been exhausted … no one was listening to me. I had been a loyal servant from the day I joined the police. I'd done all their dirty work and now when I wanted someone to listen to me, nobody would. I was left to fend for myself.'

Three years later, Joe was shocked to hear the 'official version' of what had occurred during his visit to police headquarters on 5 November. It said that he had threatened to kill the police commissioner. Joe recalled having made some wild statements but couldn't remember threatening to kill Ryan or anyone else. If he had wanted to hurt Ryan, he argued, he would have gone to his house. He knew where the commissioner lived. But this was not personal, it was professional. Police headquarters was his place of work and that was why he'd gone to see Ryan there.

But Joe's memory was blurred by prescription drugs and alcohol. While speaking to Lette Joe had threatened Ryan and others. It may have been said in the heat of the moment but it was still a threat that had to be taken seriously. The huge physique that had served Joe so well in his undercover operations made him a menacing figure. In retrospect, Joe was probably lucky that the police barring him from seeing the commissioner hadn't resorted to force.

In his book *Peter Ryan: The inside story*, written by Sue Williams, Ryan claimed a number of threats had been made against him, some of which were 'from a former police officer [Joe] that the service considered dangerous'. Not surprisingly, there was no mention in Ryan's book of the circumstances of Joe's case. To say any more would have required Ryan, as the person ultimately in charge, to have accepted some responsibility for the events that had led to Joe making his drunken threats. Similarly, Ryan found no room in his book to discuss the performance of SCIA, despite the range of serious—and sometimes criminal—allegations that had been made against it by various sources, several of which were later found to be proven (see Chapter 19).

By the end of 2001 things were at last looking up for Jessie—in September she completed her Bachelor of Social Science in Criminal Justice at the University of Western Sydney—but Joe was still trapped in a vicious spiral of anger and self-pity. His dismissal marked the end of his police career. At the same time, however, it left him free to fight back. His solicitors, Oates & Smith, now embarked on the long process of holding the New South Wales Police accountable for what they had done to Joe and Jessie.

On 13 November 2001 they lodged an application for reversal of the 181D removal order (notice of loss of commissioner's confidence) in the Industrial Relations Commission. Two weeks later, lawyers acting on behalf of Jessie filed a Statement of Claim in the District Court, claiming psychological trauma and injury as a result of the police department's negligence.

Chapter 18
'Kill Robbie'

While Jessie and Joe started looking tentatively to the future, they still struggled to put their undercover experience behind them. 'The line between duty and off-duty was always a blur,' Jessie recalled. 'Even years later, there are times when you get confused about who you are and drop back into your undercover identity. Then you realise what you are doing and ask yourself, "Am I going crazy?"'

On 19 January 2002 Joe was again pulled over by police, this time on Parramatta Road, Five Dock, by highway patrol officers. He was clocked doing 20 kilometres an hour over the 60 kilometre speed limit. There were four police at the radar trap. Joe had two passengers in his car, one of whom was Jessie. Joe denied he was doing 20 kilometres over the speed limit and got into an argument with the police, accusing them of pulling over the wrong car. (Another car was passing when Joe was waved over—it was this car that was speeding, Joe insisted.)

The police weren't interested in Joe's excuses. As far as they were concerned they had pulled over the right car: Joe had been speeding and he was going to be booked. Tempers flared on both sides as Joe and Jessie chastised the police for their 'poor customer service' and suggested they return to the Goulburn Academy for some further training. 'I know my rights,' Joe shouted. 'I was a police officer and worked at Internal Affairs.' Jessie also aggressively challenged the police.

Once again, Joe's size and belligerent manner made a tense situation much worse. The police would later claim that Joe's behaviour had been so threatening that they had feared for their safety. Eventually they gave Joe back his licence. It was Joe who urged Jessie to get back in the car and they drove off.

Three months later Joe and Jessie became engaged, but they had little time to celebrate before Joe was subpoenaed to give evidence in the trial of McArthur, Catton and Reid. Joe produced a report from his psychiatrist saying he was unfit to give evidence but this did not satisfy the Queensland authorities. In May Joe was arrested by SCIA on a Queensland warrant requesting his extradition to give evidence in Brisbane. He was charged and taken to Burwood Local Court where an extradition order was made. Joe was placed in the custody of Criminal Justice Commission officers, handcuffed and flown to Queensland. There, he was placed in the Brisbane Watch House on suicide watch.

The next day, 10 May, Joe was collected by officers of the Criminal Justice Commission and taken to the Supreme Court where he was put in a cell pending his appearance in court. 'I had felt humiliated at being handcuffed on the plane,' Joe recalled. 'Other passengers stared at me, wondering what I had done. Then at the watch-house they asked me to change into prison overalls, but they didn't fit me so I spent the night in the cells naked. I couldn't even keep my undies on. The next morning they gave me the old tracksuit I was wearing when I was arrested. They told me to put it on and I had to wear it in court.'

Meanwhile Jessie had flown up to be with him. 'They wouldn't let me give Joe a change of clothes or speak to him before he went in. When I saw him in the court in his old tracksuit, looking as if he hadn't slept, I just cried. I knew how humiliated he would have felt. I don't know why they had to treat him like that.'

In the witness box Joe was confused and frightened—he knew how corrupt police networks worked. The accused were on bail and they seemed very confident. He remembered how Michael Drury's real name had been given to those he had set up, and how he had narrowly survived being shot as a result. Now that his real name had been revealed, Joe realised how vulnerable he was.

At the end of the day Joe was bailed into the custody of the Criminal Justice Commission and taken to a nearby hotel, guarded by commission officers. In his hotel room Joe went to the bathroom and attempted to hang himself. Jessie had been allowed to stay with him and heard the thud of Joe's body hitting the floor. She ran in and found Joe unconscious, lying face down with a noose made from a towel hanging over the shower railing, which had broken from the wall, probably saving his life. The floor was covered in vomit and blood from the head cut.

Commission officers phoned for an ambulance while they tried to resuscitate Joe. He was rushed to Princess Alexandra Hospital where he told doctors that he remembered going to the bathroom and falling to the floor, but had no memory of attempting suicide. He was involuntarily admitted to the mental health ward.

The next day Joe seemed calmer, but that evening he started throwing hospital furniture around and barricaded himself on a balcony. He used his mobile phone to call a close friend in Sydney. 'I was just so depressed. I needed someone to talk to.' It took the combined efforts of Jessie and several hospital staff to persuade Joe to come in off the balcony. Speaking to doctors the next morning, Joe professed to have no memory of either the attempted hanging or the 'siege' on the balcony. The hospital released him into the care of the Witness Protection Program. He returned, heavily sedated, to the court and completed his evidence.

Jessic described him as being in a 'zombie state' as a result of the medication. Joe remembers having to splash his face with the water he had been given in a glass to stay awake. 'It was the saddest sight I had ever seen,' Jessie recalled. 'If they thought Joe was faking a breakdown when they extradited him, they couldn't think that now.'

While Joe struggled with his demons, Catton and McArthur pleaded guilty and were remanded for sentencing. Reid maintained his not guilty plea and his trial continued, with the jury finally unable to reach a verdict. A new trial date was set. On 1 June Catton was sentenced to three and a half years' jail, while McArthur was sentenced to three years' jail. It was widely regarded as the worst case of official corruption in Queensland since the close of the Fitzgerald Inquiry more than a decade earlier. Forbes Smith, director of the Investigations Directorate, Crime and Misconduct Commission (as the Criminal Justice Commission was now known), predicted that the two convicted officers would 'do their time hard'. The sentences, he said, would deter others who might be tempted to become involved in corruption.

But neither Catton nor McArthur stayed in jail for long. Six weeks after being sentenced, they were placed in work camps. In late September both were found 'relaxing with [their] families at their Brisbane southside homes'. They had been granted unsupervised home leave for several days at a time on at least two occasions. After public disclosure of their lenient treatment by Paula Doneman of the *Courier Mail*, the pair was returned to jail. The outraged corrective services minister (it was not clear whether he was outraged by the fiasco or by its disclosure) at once vowed to change the rules applying to prisoners' leave.

In Sydney, Joe was promptly served with a summons to appear before the Burwood Local Court on charges of speeding, impersonating a police officer (Joe had been removed from the police two months before the incident), intimidating a police officer and acting in an offensive manner, arising from the January traffic incident at Five Dock. To keep his depression at bay, Joe remained constantly medicated. Meanwhile, in his legal battle with the New South Wales Police, the situation was at last shifting in Joe's favour.

On 22 July 2002 lawyers for the police and Joe made their last appearance before the Industrial Relations Commission. The police were now willing to consider Joe's reinstatement as a police officer. On 28 November the new commissioner, Ken Moroney (who had been appointed commissioner after Ryan's resignation in April 2002), reversed the order removing Joe from the police. He was reinstated with 'no conditions' and compensated for his

eleven months without pay. Two years earlier it had been
Moroney, as deputy commissioner, who had suspended
Joe without pay—the first stage in the process that ended
with his dismissal. It was a bitter-sweet victory, with Joe's
relief over his reinstatement tempered by the feeling that he
should never have been dismissed to begin with.

Three months later, on 14 February 2003, the charge of
impersonating a police officer and the other charges relating
to the Five Dock traffic stop were dropped by the police.
It was the second significant victory for Joe and Jessie in
just a few months, but there was still a long way to go.
After leaving the court Jessie received a call on her mobile.
It was Chief Superintendent Bernie Aust, Commissioner
Moroney's chief of staff. He asked Jessie if she was happy
with the result.

'Yes,' Jessie replied gingerly.

'Is there anything else?' Aust asked. 'Are there any other
matters outstanding?'

'No, sir.'

'In that case take care and pass on my regards to Joe.
That's from the commissioner.'

Jessie didn't know what to make of the call. Was it a
genuine expression of the commissioner's support or simply
an attempt by the Police Executive to wash its hands of
everything?

In mid-2003 Joe was having coffee with some people he

knew from the Bankstown–Auburn area when they were joined by other locals. The conversation quickly turned to gang violence, particularly between the Adnan Darwiche and Abdul Razzak gangs. Somebody mentioned that rocket launchers stolen from the army were being offered for sale for $10,000 each. Joe's ears immediately pricked up. Since the late 1990s at least fourteen murders and around one hundred and sixty shootings had been attributed to the war between the Darwiche and Razzak crime families. Rumours that the gangs had military weapons, including rocket launchers, had been circulating for a while. Joe was aware of the rumours but this was the first time he'd heard anything to substantiate them.

While several of those around the table were known to police, Joe didn't consider them to be personally involved in the violence. Nevertheless, they knew people who were and would have known what was going on. Afterwards Joe wondered whether he was being followed by the police and whether they might even have bugged the conversation. Joe was now a convicted man on a bond. He still had a civil legal fight with the police in front of him. And he was still of interest to police because of his connection with Middle Eastern crime figures, some whom he had known since his youth.

Joe passed on the information to Task Force Gain, which was leading the police attack on Middle Eastern gang violence. A buy-bust operation—in which undercover police would buy the launchers before police arrested the seller—was discussed, but rejected. To Joe, this approach was a mistake. He wanted the rocket launchers taken off the streets before they were used. Arrests, in his view, were less urgent. They could be made later and arranged so as not to involve him or his sources. But the rocket launcher investigation was wider and more complex than he knew and Joe's involvement could have compromised other areas of the investigation.

Gain was aware that Joe was on long-term sick leave, that he had been charged over drugs and weapons offences and was in dispute with the police, although they did not know the details. Joe was also known to have a brother with a criminal record. To involve Joe would have meant asking him to act covertly within his own Muslim community—a community in which many families were related. How could he be monitored and then extracted at the end of the operation without revealing his true identity?

The risks were too great. Gain rejected the idea of using Joe, without being able to explain the reasons. The police were after one thing, but Joe was after another. His priority was to get the rocket launchers off the street as quickly as possible. The police wanted both the rocket launchers and the offenders. In fact, detectives on Task Force Gain were pursuing a number of leads that eventually resulted in one rocket launcher being recovered by the Middle Eastern gang squad, leaving another nine on the streets of Sydney. Gain finally succeeded in jailing most of the Darwiche gang, including its leader, Adnan.

*

On 14 July 2003, a year after McArthur and Catton were sentenced to jail, the retrial of Detective Reid began in the Brisbane Supreme Court. The prosecution case was strengthened by Catton's decision to give evidence against Reid. It took the jury ten hours to reach a decision, but this time there was no doubt in their mind: Reid was convicted of selling ecstasy and sentenced to six years' jail.

While the charges against McArthur, Catton and Reid were making their way through the courts, Josh Sexton pleaded guilty to supplying drugs. He also agreed to cooperate with the Criminal Justice Commission. Sexton was placed on twelve months' probation. Peter Whitten was convicted of drug trafficking and sentenced to three years' jail while Russell Lemberg was admitted to hospital and is believed to have died of a drug overdose.

Joe and Jessie's relationship had endured some stormy periods. For a time they had separated, but the months they spent apart had shown them that they wanted and needed to be together. In January 2004 Jessie and Joe married, but even their wedding was not without its difficulties. Some of the invited guests knew them by their undercover names only. Few in Joe's extended family knew he was still in the police and most only knew Jessie by her undercover name. None knew she was a police officer. Jessie's family knew she and Joe were undercover police, but knew Joe only by his undercover name.

Two months after the wedding, Jessie retired from the police medically unfit and received a 'special risk benefit'—a benefit paid to police who have been injured on duty. Jessie had been off sick for several months with recurring bouts of depression and anxiety, but it was Reid's retrial and the effect it had on Joe that made her realise she'd had enough.

More bad news was to follow. A few months after she retired, Jessie learnt that her mother had been diagnosed with breast cancer. With the help of surgery and chemotherapy, her mother recovered. Jessie remains convinced that the cancer had been triggered by the stress of supporting her and Joe.

Meanwhile Joe struggled for another two years to rebuild his career in the police. He returned to work several times, but each attempt was followed by a long period of sick leave. In December 2003 Joe's doctor had assessed him as being 'unlikely to successfully return to any form of police work at any time in the foreseeable future'. There were many reasons for this but the biggest challenge for Joe was how to separate himself from his undercover identity. Joe and his doctors both grappled with the question of how to 'kill' Robbie, the undercover name he most closely identified with.

During the years he had wrestled with depression, Joe had always found refuge in the character of 'Robbie'. Robbie wasn't him, but at the same time he was Robbie. With his 'real' career so uncertain, Joe often visited Kings Cross, assuming the role of Robbie. He visited the old haunts and mixed with many of the characters he knew from those earlier years, feeling oddly at home in the needle-strewn alleys and litter-filled doorways of Kings Cross.

The character of Robbie was an inseparable part of him. Using Robbie's name, he continued to train in the gyms he had trained in for more than eight years, tormented by the thought of revealing to all those who had known him as Robbie—many of them honest and law-abiding people—that Robbie was a fraud. How could he explain to them that he had betrayed their trust and friendship over all those years?

Joe had used steroids continually from 1996 until the end of 2000 when he went 'cold turkey' and gave them up. At the height of his panic over the criminal charges against him, he relapsed and used steroids for about ten weeks during 2001. Two and a half years later he used them again for around six weeks, but has not touched steroids since.

In early 2005 Joe went on sick leave from the police for the last time.

Chapter 19
Reform

Joe never claimed to be blameless, but his mistakes pale compared with those of a police hierarchy that consistently refused to acknowledge—let alone rectify— entrenched problems in both undercover operations and internal affairs. In almost every instance it was fear of media scrutiny, over which it would have little or no control, that prompted concessions or admissions which until then had been stubbornly withheld.

On 10 May 2000, after Joe's arrest was leaked to the media, Deputy Commissioner Ken Moroney issued a statement declaring that both he 'and the Commissioner of Police had full confidence in Commander Mal Brammer as head of Special Crime and Internal Affairs'. At the time at least five serious internal investigations were under way into the operations and management of SCIA. The actions of Brammer were central to each. In addition, three more formal investigations were about to begin. Each one found significant shortcomings in SCIA.

One long-running investigation, codenamed Shillingstone, found that Brammer had a 'manifest conflict of interest' in an operation undertaken by SCIA; had perverted the course of justice by improperly arranging for the assessment and initiation of an internal investigation against a police officer; had breached the *Protected Disclosures Act*, and had 'improperly engaged in the assessment process of an internal complaint' made by a police superintendent.

Another, codenamed Banks, made adverse findings against seven SCIA officers. Criminal charges of perverting the course of justice were considered against several of them but after advice from the Director of Public Prosecutions, Nicholas Cowdery, no charges were laid. Managerial action, however, was taken against some officers.

In February 2003 the New South Wales Police Integrity Commission (PIC) released the results of its 2000–02 Operation Malta inquiry into allegations that senior police had undermined a team of crime management reformers. While the commission did not recommend action against any individual, it expressed the opinion that 'As Commander of the Service's internal investigations unit, Brammer had a responsibility to ensure there was scrupulous adherence to the principle of impartial investigation by his unit. This did not happen.' In the commission's view there was evidence to support the allegation that 'Brammer was affected by bias in his investigation of [Ken] Seddon and the Crime Management Support Unit' and 'There was a lack of fairness in Brammer's investigation'. The commission concluded that it was 'not appropriate for Brammer to conduct the investigation personally.' It was also critical of Ryan, accusing him of several errors of judgement.

No inquiry was more embarrassing to SCIA than the one into Task Force Bax. Set up in 1996, Bax was an attempt to infiltrate the gangs fighting for control of the Kings Cross drug trade in the wake of the Wood Royal Commission. The task force was disbanded after twenty months when it became the subject of a corruption investigation by SCIA and the PIC.

In his book, *Peter Ryan: The inside story*, Ryan claimed personal leadership of the Bax operation: 'It was set to be one of the most daring operations ever undertaken by a Commissioner of Police in Australia ... Ryan had led a massive covert surveillance program.' The operation was a 'triumph', Ryan declared.

The truth was rather different. A PIC inquiry found that one Bax drug investigation had been compromised and that there were managerial shortcomings in the conduct of the task force. One member of Bax, Detective Robert 'Squeaker' Irwin and a detective colleague, Craig 'Snidely Whiplash'

McDonald (not attached to Bax), were charged with and jailed for perverting the course of justice and lying to the Police Integrity Commission. The head of Bax, Superintendent Geoff Wegg, was charged with lying to the commission, but at trial the judge directed his aquittal.

Several members of Bax sued the force over its handling of the investigation into the task force. Ten years later, in December 2007, the New South Wales Police and government settled the claims of nine former Bax officers. The terms of settlement were not disclosed but were rumoured to have included a total payout of around $5 million, making it one of the biggest ever made in response to litigation by police officers against the department.

Given these investigations and other allegations against SCIA, Jessie's 2001 internal police complaint about Joe's and her treatment and the management of SCIA should not have come as a surprise to the Police Executive. Jessie's complaint led to the establishment of two strike forces: Tumen and Sibutu. Unlike a police task force, which was generally long-running with wide terms of reference, and could be vulnerable to corruption, a strike force was narrowly focused, short-term, and intended to be disbanded once the investigation was over. Tumen focused on the treatment of Joe and Jessie, while Sibutu examined broader management and personnel practices.

Strike Force Tumen spent a year investigating almost forty separate issues. It made adverse findings in sixteen matters against at least five SCIA officers and general adverse findings in about twenty matters. In some cases there was overlap between the findings against specific officers and the general adverse findings. In a handful of cases the inquiry was unable to determine the truth of the matter because one or more SCIA officers involved declined to be interviewed and/or records were missing.

Among other things the strike force identified a failure to exercise proper supervision; untruthfulness; not providing timely psychological assessments of Joe and Jessie; conflicts of interest; misuse of authority; and the use of incorrect procedures. It also found serious shortcomings in even the most fundamental aspects of criminal investigation. An interview with Jessie by SCIA was found to be unprofessional. There had been a failure to disclose the 'nature, scope and details of allegations, lack of interview preparation, disjointed interview ... inappropriate questions, inappropriate comments on ... answers [given], [and] oppression'. Generally, the strike force found there had been a failure to provide proper training and psychological assessment, and that management had been inadequate. Poor communication and lack of feedback from supervisors exacerbated problems for operatives in the field.

The failure to ensure reliable record keeping highlighted 'the ad hoc and outdated system of recording internal investigations that existed at SCIA'.

One of the matters about which the investigation was unable to reach a conclusion was whether senior police had condoned Joe's use of steroids. One officer who worked with Joe over several years admitted that he knew Joe used steroids, but said he thought they were prescribed. He said he had mentioned this to others at SCIA, but those 'others' said they could not recall it being mentioned.

While Strike Force Tumen was in progress, at least five other undercover police engaged in civil actions against the department (but not against SCIA) claimed the use of illegal drugs—including heroin and cocaine—had been sanctioned by senior police. In a few cases it was claimed they had sanctioned the use of steroids. One, Tim Rochford, who had worked undercover for six years during the late 1980s and early 1990s, told ABC TV's *Stateline* in 2005 that they were expected to use drugs in order to appear credible. 'We were instructed very early on in our undercover work that if we were ever asked in court if we took drugs, we would have to not acknowledge that—we would have to say we didn't.' Another operative claimed that in 1998 her two-week undercover course in Puckapunyal, Victoria, included 'smoking marijuana and hash'.

Several senior SCIA officers, including the commander, Mal Brammer, had known Joe from his years at the drug squad. It is difficult to believe that anyone who saw him during his time with SCIA would not have suspected that Joe was using steroids. In fact, some did. On 29 December

2000 a drug squad detective and his partner were patrolling Parramatta when they noticed Joe and a companion walking along Church Street. The detective recorded the sighting. Despite it being dark, he noted: 'POI [person of interest] appeared to be overly muscular. My opinion based on drug experience is that [his build] was steroid assisted.'

Tumen investigated Joe and Jessie's allegation that their supervisor, Sergeant Graeme Pickering, had compromised the Queensland operation and their safety through his behaviour and relationship with the landlady at the Blacks Beach safe house.

In his initial interview Pickering explained that he and the landlady became 'friends, I suppose'. Later he admitted that 'we might've gone to dinner or something one night ... at the local pub'. However, he repeatedly denied having a sexual relationship with her. He also denied that his relationship with the landlady had caused a conflict for him or that it could have compromised the operation or the safety of the undercover operatives he was supervising. Later Pickering changed his story. He admitted to having a sexual affair with the landlady. Asked how many times they had had sex, he replied, 'I don't know', it was more than once, and 'less than 100 [times]'. According to Pickering, he had lied to avoid causing 'trouble and personal embarrassment'.

Tumen investigators found that Pickering's relationship with the landlady 'had the potential to compromise the whole operation' and raised 'safety issues' for the undercover operatives. Findings of 'failure to exercise proper supervision', 'improper association' and 'untruthfulness' were also made against him. Despite these findings and subsequent disciplinary action, Pickering was soon promoted to the rank of inspector, a rank he still holds. For a period he was acting commander—at the rank of superintendent—at Sydney's Northern Beaches local area command.

These findings against Pickering—whose job with SCIA was to root out corruption and ensure professional standards were upheld—did not appear to worry the new commissioner, Ken Moroney, who saw them as no impediment to promotion. Responding to a January 2007 *Daily Telegraph* article, 'Cop's under-covers sex romp', by Janet Fife-Yeomans, a spokesman for Commissioner Moroney explained, 'At the time of [Pickering's] promotion the matter was finalised and there was nothing further to preclude this officer from promotion'. The matter of Pickering's misconduct might have been 'finalised' but Joe and Jessie were now in the seventh year of their fight for justice.

Tumen also reviewed the covert operations that targeted Detective Inspector Deborah Wallace and Assistant Commissioner Clive Small. It found that a report by Wallace herself, in which she outlined the seeminglyunexplained wealth and suspicious activities of an aerobics instructor who worked at a western suburbs gym and her strip club-owning husband, had led to Wallace being targeted. Records concerning the surveillance of Wallace were found to be either missing or non-existent. Tumen did confirm, however, that the operation lasted for seven months. Yet, remarkably, none of the senior SCIA officers involved was able to recall Jessie being told to look at Wallace; several were unable to even recall the operation. Reporting its findings, Tumen stated: 'Strike force investigators suspect the operation was not bona fide or justified but are unable to substantiate this assertion.' It emphasised that there were no grounds to indicate that Wallace had acted inappropriately.

Tumen made no adverse finding in respect of the SCIA investigation into allegations made by Neddy Smith of an inappropriate relationship between crime boss Michael Hurley and Small. Unlike Wallace, Small was never interviewed about his alleged association with Hurley or the surveillance of the Woolwich Pier Hotel. News of the surveillance only reached Small in early 2000 when he was contacted by a reporter who had been leaked the information.

The surveillance of Small came to the notice of Detective Inspector Michael Drury, who had become Australia's highest-profile undercover cop after being shot through the window of his Chatswood home by Melbourne killer Christopher 'Rent-a-Kill' Flannery. Drury expressed grave reservations about the Small operation. In a 2005 statement to Joe's and Jessie's lawyers, Drury wrote:

I am aware of the circumstances surrounding the investigation of the alleged corrupt activities of Assistant Commissioner Clive Small ... I have serious concerns about the investigational foundation of this case as no intelligence or evidence was ever forthcoming into the alleged corrupt activities of Assistant Commissioner Clive Small ... This again reflects poorly upon [name deleted], [name deleted] and [name deleted].

Tumen was never told about the surveillance of Peter Ryan and his wife in late 2000. There was no official record and Joe refused to cooperate with investigators. Those in SCIA who knew of the operation had every incentive to conceal it. By any reasonable analysis there can be only one conclusion: the operation against Ryan was an abuse of power and proof of an SCIA leadership out of control.

The other strike force set up as a result of Jessie's complaints, Strike Force Sibutu, identified serious shortcomings in the way SCIA handled internal investigations. It found that SCIA operated an ad hoc and outdated records system that allowed some investigation files to go missing, while others necessary for the integrity of operations never existed at all. Several investigators given temporary promotion at SCIA, including some appointed to the ranks of inspector and superintendent, were found 'not [to] have the capability to properly discharge the functions of the positions they held'.

While the police department's centralised undercover and surveillance unit had—presumably with the approval of the Police Executive—adopted the recommendations of the 1996 Kaldas review of undercover operatives, SCIA had not.

Despite his documented failings as head of SCIA, Brammer proposed in 2000 that all undercover and surveillance operatives and facilities be placed under his command. He claimed that corruption existed within the surveillance and undercover command and wanted SCIA to deal with it.

A meeting chaired by Assistant Commissioner Christine Nixon was held at police headquarters to discuss the proposal. Assistant Commissioner Clive Small and Superintendent Nick Kaldas, both of Crime Agencies, and senior representatives of the surveillance and undercover command attended the meeting. Despite the serious allegations being made by SCIA, not one of that command's senior officers attended. The meeting was not given a single example of so-called corruption, nor was there any reference to the operational problems within SCIA's covert unit. It was a naked grab for power. Nixon reported the results of the meeting to Deputy Commissioner Moroney. Brammer did not get his way. In fact SCIA's covert unit was closed down.

Arguably the most damning finding against SCIA was that five years after the Wood Royal Commission it had not acted on Justice Wood's detailed recommendations about the use of undercover operatives (see Appendix 2). This was despite guarantees given by the police commissioner that all recommendations had been fully implemented.

Ryan became commissioner of the New South Wales Police in September 1996 as the Wood Royal Commission was winding up its hearings and preparing its final reports. He was given more power than any previous commissioner—a fact not lost on Ryan. As Sue Williams wrote in *Peter Ryan: The inside story*, '[S]uddenly unfettered by civilian overseers, [Ryan] had become possibly the most powerful Police Commissioner in history.' But within two years the reform framework proposed by the Wood Royal Commission and accepted by both Ryan and the government had been abandoned. How could this have happened in an organisation that had just been the subject of a four-year $100 million royal commission?

No sooner had the commission's final reports been released than Ryan told *Sun Herald* journalist Darren Goodsir in a September 1997 interview: 'What I have to do is say to the cops: "Never mind this reform business ... concentrate on getting crime down".' It was a message he spread far and wide.

After the royal commission the New South Wales government appointed an auditor to report annually on the progress of police reform. In 1998 the premier, Bob Carr, formally dropped the government's promise of reform, declaring: 'It is time for police to put the Wood Commission behind them and get down to the business of solving crime.'

Any doubts that police reform was off the government's agenda were dispelled by its response to the first strategic audit of the reform process. For twelve months the government refused to release the report. Then in mid-February 2001 in a *Sydney Morning Herald* article headlined 'Ryan's Push for Free Hand on Reforms', the commissioner complained that 'I get oversighted [sic] by people who haven't got a bloody clue ... They couldn't run a chook raffle.' These people who 'couldn't run a chook raffle' were the same people who just a few years earlier had supported his appointment and whose reform agenda he had publicly embraced in order to get the job.

The first strategic audit report found that although 'some real progress had been achieved ... [reform was] systematically limited', fragmented, slow, and in some areas had come to a halt. A *Sydney Morning Herald* article titled 'The Minister, the Commissioner and the PIC', quoted the premier as having dismissed the report's findings, describing them as 'management jargon'. The strategic audit findings for the second and third years—which identified further deficiencies in the reform process—received even shorter shrift. The final insult came from the then police minister, Michael Costa. He released the last audit report two days before Christmas 2002, ensuring it would go unnoticed by almost everyone.

That the Labor government should have been so keen to wash its hands of the audit should have come as no surprise to anyone. This was a government that, from its earliest days in office, had set about reclaiming the law and order issue from the conservatives. Determined to be seen as being tough on crime, Carr and a string of police ministers proved adept at massaging clear-up statistics while paying lip service to the sort of essential structural reforms that had been advocated by the Wood Royal Commission. But, as the final audit report spelt out, it wasn't just the government that was at fault. 'The main factor contributing to stalled progress', it said, 'was the failure of the [Police] Executive to manage reform strategically.'

One incident, more than any other, demonstrated the flawed judgement at the highest levels of the police that enabled the managerial and operational bungles of SCIA to continue. It came to light as part of an internal investigation known as Operation Shillingstone. In August 1997 Commissioner Ryan had sought 'advice' from Brammer over a series of complaints made against Brammer himself by Detective Sergeant John Edlund and the New South Wales MP John Hatton. Hatton, then the independent member for the South Coast, was a long-recognised anti-corruption campaigner who, five years earlier, had been instrumental in setting up the Wood Royal Commission.

Operation Shillingstone found that Ryan's decision to seek 'advice' from Brammer was understandable given his recent appointment as commissioner, his 'lack of knowledge of the various involved parties' and his recent appointment of Brammer to 'a most trusted position within the Service [Special Crime and Internal Affairs]'. However, that finding appears to ignore the fact that in doing so he disregarded written warnings from Edlund, Hatton and Assistant commissioner Christine Nixon (who went on to become the commissioner of the Victoria Police), in which all three expressed 'unambiguous concerns' about asking Brammer's advice on how to handle a formal complaint against himself.

In his advice to Ryan, Brammer wrote, 'Given the history of Mr Hatton's resolute pursuit of myself [and others who questioned the veracity of his perceptions] … it is my submission that any further inquiry is an absolute waste of time and effort.'

In accepting Brammer's advice not to investigate the complaints by Hatton and Edlund, Ryan was oblivious to, or chose to ignore, a blatant conflict of interest that ought to have excluded Brammer from any role in assessing the complaint. That such an abuse of basic investigative procedure should have been allowed to happen, not by an anonymous mid-level officer but by the commissioner himself, was telling proof that the Police Executive was not fit to manage its own reform.

Peter Ryan had been given the equivalent of a 'blank cheque' on his appointment as commissioner of police. But the cheque bounced: first on Ryan himself, who was effectively sacked by the government in 2002, and second on the New South Wales Police. Vital reforms which Ryan had promised to implement in their entirety were either never begun or allowed to peter out half finished. The fault lay heavily with the government, which was happy to see the issue of police corruption and inefficiency off the front pages, even at the expense of much-needed reform. In prematurely claiming success for the disastrous operation to clean up Task Force Bax, Ryan declared: 'People seemed to have learned nothing from the Royal Commission.'

The two people for whom this remark was patently true were Ryan himself and his deputy, Mal Brammer.

Chapter 20
A new start

As their civil actions against the New South Wales Police worked their way through the courts, Joe and Jessie struggled to find a new future for themselves. In 2003 Joe made his first tentative move to return to Islam. It had given him moral strength as a young man and he needed that now more than ever. 'I had lost my faith and I had to cleanse my body and mind. I wanted to be the person I used to be. When I was on beats, I gave lectures at school to kids. Those were happy days. I had let my parents down. They were wondering what they had done to deserve all this. The answer was they hadn't done anything. It was my fault and I had to make up for it—to make them proud of me once again.'

Returning to his faith was not easy. For nearly a decade the life Joe had led as an undercover cop had been the antithesis of everything he'd been brought up to believe in. But Joe is now a practising conservative Muslim. He no longer takes steroids, drinks alcohol or smokes.

The years of steroid abuse have done long-term damage to Joe's health. In 2006, after passing blood, he was admitted to Westmead Hospital with kidney failure. 'I'd known something was wrong for some time but this frightened the hell out of me. The doctors told me I wasn't going to die, but I knew I was in trouble. There was no quick fix.' Joe was placed on dialysis and kept in hospital for a week. After he was released, his dialysis treatment continued for three months. Over the next year Joe's condition appeared to stabilise, then early in 2007 his kidneys failed again. Readmitted to hospital, he was discharged after four days but remained on medication and needed a special diet.

His and Jessie's claims for psychological trauma and injury against the New South Wales Police were set down for a ten-week hearing starting in July 2007, but as the date approached the case was settled out of court. Joe and Jessie were happy with the result. On 10 August Joe retired from the police medically unfit. Except for six shifts during early 2005, Joe had been on sick leave for the previous two and a half years.

The same month Peter Ryan's successor, Police Commissioner Ken Moroney, called the pair to his office and presented them with identical awards. One was a Commissioner's Commendation for Service, 'Awarded for outstanding and meritorious performance of duty as a member of the New South Wales Police whilst on secondment with the Queensland Crime and Misconduct Commission'.

The other was a Certificate of Recognition 'of [her/his] contribution to Operation Undercover Policing in New South Wales' which acknowledged their 'contribution and commitment to achieving cost effective, ethical crime reduction'.

The professionalism for which Joe and Jessie were commended was disappointingly absent from the certificates themselves, which were riddled with spelling mistakes. But after years of being let down by the police hierarchy, Jessie and Joe saw something oddly appropriate in the shoddiness of those awards.

Both had now left the police. The ceremony in the commissioner's office offered the pair a chance to draw a line under careers that had started brilliantly, only to end in humiliation and disappointment. As they walked away for the last time from police headquarters, Joe and Jessie could finally start thinking about the future: a future in which they wouldn't constantly be looking over their shoulder; a future in which they would no longer have to pretend to be people they were not.

Joe and Jessie badly wanted children and they were thrilled to discover in late 2007 that Jessie was going to have twins. In June 2008 Jessie was admitted to hospital suffering from dangerously high blood pressure. The twins were born early the next morning by emergency caesarean, but severe haemorrhaging meant Jessie had to undergo two further bouts of surgery. It was several days before she was well enough to care for them. Once they were allowed home, Jessie quickly recovered. From now on the twins would be the focus of their lives. 'We knew that we wanted children,' says Jessie, 'but we didn't realise how much joy they would give us. It was the twins, much more than the court settlement, that allowed us to put our former lives behind us.'

After leaving the police Jessie completed a degree in teaching and started work as a primary school teacher—a career that was soon interrupted by the birth of the twins.

In December 2007 Joe took a job as transport supervisor in a haulage firm. He enjoyed the work but seven months later was forced to give up when his condition worsened and he was readmitted to hospital with high blood pressure and kidney failure. This time Joe was told he would need long-term dialysis treatment: nine-hour sessions every second day. His kidneys were too damaged to recover and Joe took his place on the State's ever-increasing waiting list for a kidney transplant. The strict conditions of his diet meant that Joe could rarely eat out and was unable to travel far from a hospital.

Joe received his dialysis treatment at home, helped by Jessie, who had to be trained to look after him: 'Having the treatment at home is much better than going to the hospital, especially now that we have the twins, but it's still very difficult. I can't wait for Joe to have the transplant but we both know that could be years off. Until then it's something we just have to learn to live with.'

Says Joe: 'For a guy who was worried about getting killed and who tried to take his life a couple of times, it was ironic that I had to wait for someone to die so I could have their kidney and live a normal life. I didn't want anyone to die, but I was desperate for a kidney.'

No one had to die and Joe got his transplant. Mark, the longtime partner of one of Jessie's sisters, came forward to offer Joe one of his kidneys. Mark had known for some time that Joe was sick, but it was not until after Joe and Jessie had retired from the police in 2007 that he discovered what the pair had been through and how ill Joe was. Over the next few years he saw Joe's condition deteriorate. Aware that Joe might die before his turn came up on the transplant program, Mark had himself tested to see whether he could give Joe one of his kidneys. The tests showed that they were compatible and in March 2010 Joe and Mark underwent transplant operations. 'At first it was a hard thing to contemplate,' Mark recalls. 'But once I realised that I would be giving two young babies [Joe and Jessie's twins] a father and Jessie the life of her husband, the decision was easy. It was a small sacrifice when I considered the impact this would have on a whole family.' They were not the only ones to benefit, he says. 'It has brought me closer to Joe and Jessie and their families. I discovered how much more rewarding it is to participate in life rather than simply be a spectator.'

*

Unlike many other police, Joe finds it impossible to look back on his career as an undercover cop with any satisfaction. 'What have I done? I've cheated, lied and deceived people. I've ruined marriages, ruined lives, ruined relationships, ruined [the] health of other people, not to mention my own. But have I made a difference to the problem of illegal drugs on the street? I don't think so. There are more drugs out there now than when I started.'

Both of them know that Joe's alter ego needs to be killed off before the real Joe—husband of Jessie and father of the twins—will ever be free. But deep down he believes that 'Robbie' will always be with him. He accepts the assessment of the police psychologist, Jennifer Lette, that 'Robbie will never be gone from [Joe's real name deleted] life ... some integration of the two personalities may be the final result.'

If Joe can never escape his undercover life, he is at least reconciled to where it has taken him. 'Faith has become my

anchor. Changing my ways saved my life, gave me a beautiful wife and two beautiful children. I have everything to
live for.'

Appendix 1

Joe's working list of drugs, street names and prices, circa 1996

During the 1990s the New South Wales Drug Enforcement Agency regularly recorded the street names and prices of different drugs. Roughly every six months a list of commonly used names and average prices—from bulk supply to street deals—was compiled as a reference for police involved in investigating the drug trade.

Joe's working notes, reproduced below, are drawn from a 1996 reference list. The list was intended to be indicative rather than definitive. Prices could be affected by a range of variables such as purity, availability and location; whether the buy was a sample to facilitate larger buys; and whether the buyers and sellers were conducting a one-off transaction or had an ongoing business relationship (one-off transactions were likely to be more expensive).

During the mid to late 1990s the Cabramatta drug market provided heroin of higher purity and at a cheaper price than the Kings Cross drug market. Kings Cross provided heroin of higher purity and at a cheaper price than was available in other suburbs in south and south-west Sydney. Cocaine was more readily available and cheaper across Sydney's eastern and inner suburbs than in Sydney's west or in cities and country towns elsewhere in New South Wales.

The biggest variation in price occurred in amphetamines. Even bulk sales could be of street-level purity, probably around 3–4 per cent, while others could be as high as 18 per cent. A pound of street-level speed could cost as little as $18,000 while a pound of high-quality speed could cost as much as $55,000.

Heroin   Depressants

Smack, Hammer, Rock

Powder : white, cream, beige or brown.
pink or white rocks.

Taste (fifty)	0.1 - 0.2g	$50
Hundred	0.3 - 0.4g	$100
½ Weight	0.4g	$160
Weight	0.6 - 0.8g	$350/450
5 weight	5 grams	$1500/1850
10 grams		$3000/3500
½ Ounce 0^z	14 grams	$4000/5000
1 Ounce 0^z	28 grams	$8500/9500
1 pound uncut.	454g	$85000/125000

N^{0} 4
N^{0} 3

<u>Cocaine</u>:   <u>Stimulants</u>

Coke, Snow, blow, Crack & Rock.

<u>White Powder</u> : will have a crystal
   appearance when in pure form.
   white + cream rocks.

½ Gram	$100
1 Gram	$200
10 Gram bag	$1800/2000
¼ Ounce bag (7 grams)	$1000
1 ounce bag (28 grams)	$4000/4500
½ Kilo (500 grams)	$60 000/65000
1 Kilo (1000 grams)	$110000/130000

<u>Crack</u> :   Glass gar filled with
   Coke and higher ratio
   of bi carb soda.
   Placed into pot of boiling
   water. Solidifies into
   a grey rock.

AMPHETAMINE :   Stimulants

Speed, Goey, Ice
liquid form   ox blood.

Powder : white, beige or brown
        (depending on purity).
liquid - red, brown or orange
Crystal - (Ice) clear of milky appearace

1 gram		$90/120
¼ ounce	(7 grams)	$450 - 500
1 ounce	(28 grams)	$1100/1600
1 lb (from source) (16 ounce)		$9000/12000
½ lb	(8 ounces)	$7000/8000
1 lb (from retail)		$15000/18000
1 kilo		$25000/35000
1 vial (1ml ox)		$80/150

<u>MDMA</u>: (Ecstasy) <u>Hallucinogen</u>

<u>Eccy's, E's, XTC, love drug.</u>

<u>Powder</u> white, tablets/capsules -
white, red and orange.

1 Tablet	$40/50
Moderate dose	35/85 mgm
High dose	85/100 mgm

| 1 Capsule | $35/50 |
| 25+ (Bulk Tablets) | $20/30 |

L.S.D (lysergic Acid Diethylamide)

Hallucinogens

Acid, Tab's, tickets, trips.

Coloured blotting paper

1-100 Tab $10/20
100-1000 tabs $4/10

Current,   white rabbits, Bart.
       smiling faces, strawberries

<u>Cannabis</u> Depresent / Hallucingen /
                    intoxicant

Grass, Head, Pot, Smoko.

G. V. M.

1 deal (1 gram)		$20-25
1 ounce (28 grams)		$300/700
1 lb (16 oz) leaf		$1500/2200
1 lb Head		$3500/4500
10 lbs		$28000/35000
50 lbs		$75000/100000
Imported	1 kilo (compressed brick)	$7000/12000
Resin	1 deal (1 gr)	$20/50
	1 ounce	$450/600
	1 kilo	$8000/12500
Oil	1 deal (1 gr)	$50
	1 ounce	$400/600
	1 kilo	$10 000/14000

APPENDIX 1

Weights:

1 Lbs = 454 grams = 16 oz

1 kg = 2.2 Lbs

1 oz = 28.4 grams.

Appendix 2

Wood Royal Commission recommendations regarding the use of undercover operatives

In its report Royal Commission into the New South Wales Police Service, Final Report, Volume II, the Wood Royal Commission made a number of recommendations relating to undercover policing. Broadly, the recommendations fell into two categories: legislative changes to ensure the legality of various aspects of undercover operations and 'the development of guidelines for the use of long-term undercover operatives'. The latter are listed below:

USE OF UNDERCOVER OPERATIVES

7.80 The desirability of the use of serving police in any long-term undercover capacity has in recent times come to be seriously questioned. The problems identified relate to the corrupting nature of this form of work, the long-term psychological consequences attributable to the stress involved arising out of the need to assume a very different identity, and to engage in conduct which is often the antithesis of the values appropriately held by a police officer.

7.81 So far as the Commission is aware, the NSW Police Service seems not to have used its members in long-term undercover operations. For that reason, the Commission merely expresses the need, in the event of any task force or agency deciding to engage in this form of activity, for the Service to develop and carefully implement guidelines which provide for:

- intense vigilance to ensure that the undercover operative is not corrupted by the circumstances of the operation, and in particular, is not expected to personally inject or use drugs;
- psychological profiling of undercover officers;
- careful selection of operatives based on their experience and suitability for the work;
- careful training for undercover officers including where possible 'on the job training';
- meticulous planning of operations including assessment

of the risk and/or necessity for the use of an undercover operative;

- regular review by qualified staff to confirm the suitability of the officer to continue in undercover work; and
- rotation of duties, and counselling where stress is observed, or the operative is moved to another job.